# CLASSIC FRENCH COOKING

By Anne Willan
Illustrated by Susan Alcantarilla

SAINSBURY · WALKER BOOKS

*For Fernand Chambrette and Claude Vauguet*
*La Varenne chefs*
*in gratitude and friendship*

SAINSBURY CLASSIC COOKBOOKS
Series editor: Jill Norman
Designer: Jim Bunker

Published exclusively for
J Sainsbury plc
Stamford Street London SE1 9LL
by Walker Books Ltd
184-192 Drummond Street
London NW1 3HP

First published 1986

Text © 1986 Anne Willan
Illustrations © 1986 Walker Books Ltd

ISBN 0-7445-0654-9

# CONTENTS

# INTRODUCTION

My first introduction to classic French cooking was taken in a Yorkshire kitchen at the behest of our fat old cook. It was she who explained how to hold the knife to chop parsley; who taught me how to make gravy and then taste it for seasoning. On baking day I beat the eggs into pound cake and rolled the dough for custard tarts. Her cooking, of course, was very English, but it was my first lesson that classic principles are universal.

Fifteen years later, when I went to France, I found to my delight that the French quite simply pay more attention to cooking than anyone else. That's why they have developed the most varied repertoire of dishes in the West. Homely quiche, costly tournedos, vinaigrette dressing, petits fours, bouillabaisse – all are clearly identified with France. Common to all is a meticulous attention to detail, to obtaining the right ingredients and using the correct technique.

In this book I've begun with the basics: the sauces which form part of so many typical French dishes. Then I go on to explore the dishes themselves, the mousses, the ragoûts and soufflés, each with its own characteristics and, often, special piece of cooking equipment. (Desserts and pastries are to come in a later volume.)

Few of the recipes are classic in the sense that they can be found in Escoffier, for today new ideas and a different lifestyle have led to a lighter, more colourful approach. Sauces are less rich, salads are a popular first course, electric machines proliferate. The cooking techniques and principles used to make the recipes, however, are unchanged and the first step is to pin them down. What meats are suitable for a sauté and what size should they be cut? What are the attributes of good crêpes and how should they be stored? Armed with this knowledge, the second step towards the dishes themselves is easy. In each chapter the recipes form a pattern, following the guidelines in the opening text. The third step is for you, the cook, to create your own variations on the originals. I've made some suggestions: for instance, duck instead of pork can be braised with apricots, and all manner of flavourings can take the place of ham and cheese in the quiche Lorraine. To experiment and improvise, while following classic principles and techniques, is the name of the game. It is then that the fun begins. Cooking should never be routine, but a personal reflection of the season, the ingredients and the cook's individual taste.

*Anne Willan*

## 1

# FLOUR-BASED SAUCES

Name any ingredient – steak, sweetbreads, sole, salsify – and there will be at least one, and possibly a dozen, French sauces that go with it. Sauces add richness to roast meats or reinforce the delicate flavours of fish and poultry; bind croquettes or enliven plain boiled vegetables. Luckily the cook needs to know only a few sauces by heart. Once the principles for making the three classic flour-based sauces – white, velouté and brown – are established, a whole repertoire can be built around them by the simple addition of a flavouring. Sauce aurore, for instance, is the name given to a white sauce once a little tomato purée is added, and a brown sauce becomes sauce bordelaise with red wine, shallot and bone marrow.

Distinct as they are, the three flour-based sauces share many attributes. Flavour should be concentrated so a small amount highlights the food it accompanies. The key is careful seasoning – a sauce should be tasted often during cooking. With stock*-based sauces, long simmering is important so they mellow and reduce. All sauces should be smoothed by diligent whisking as they come to the boil. The classic whisk for sauces is made of metal with a plump handle that is easy to grip. The more loops of wire, the less stirring needed. Use a heavy pan with a thick base and sloping sides so that the whisk reaches every corner.

The gloss of the sauce is improved by working through a fine conical 'chinois' strainer at the end of cooking. Correct consistency depends on the recipe, but the trend nowadays is towards lighter sauces which only just coat the back of a spoon. Too thick a sauce glues the tongue, but too thin a sauce dilutes the whole dish.

### WHITE SAUCE

White sauce is the most versatile and is therefore often the first serious challenge for the aspiring cook. To make the classic 'roux' – the thickener of butter and flour – for white sauce, butter is melted in the pan and flour stirred in with a whisk. Proportions, about half the weight of flour to butter, ensure the roux spreads in the pan and bubbles evenly. A roux must be thoroughly cooked, stirring for 1-2 minutes, so the finished sauce does not taste of uncooked flour. However, don't let the roux start to brown.

Then milk is added – do this quickly, whisking hard so there is no problem with lumps. (If any do form, simply pour the sauce through a strainer.) If the milk is scalded first, it shortens the time you spend whisking while the sauce comes to the boil. At boiling point the sauce thickens and is left to simmer for 2-3 minutes – white sauce scorches easily and is never cooked for long.

White sauce is the only sauce made deliberately in various consistencies by varying the proportion of flour and butter to milk. Thick sauce is used for binding mixtures such as croquettes, medium for coating, and thin as a base for soup or when other binding ingredients such as egg yolks or cheese are added.

*For more detailed information about terms marked with an asterisk, see glossary p.88.*

## VELOUTE SAUCE

Velouté sauce, made with stock\* instead of milk, is also thickened with a roux but the sauce itself is cooked somewhat differently. Less roux is added at the beginning of cooking, so that the sauce starts out quite thin. It is left to simmer, stirring occasionally, anywhere from 10 to 45 minutes. During this time the sauce reduces, so the consistency thickens while the flavour mellows.

Velouté often appears as an integral part of a dish when the stock used as a cooking liquid is later thickened as a sauce. Typical is veal blanquette (p.47), where once the meat is cooked the stock is strained, thickened and reheated with the meat so that the flavours blend. Velouté is particularly suited to white meats, poultry and fish because it will heighten flavours which might otherwise be bland. Good stock is essential for a good velouté and little other seasoning is necessary, though a squeeze of lemon juice is often an improvement. At the end of cooking these sauces may be further enriched – white sauce by adding cream, and velouté with both cream and egg yolks, a mixture which must be combined with care as it curdles easily.

## BROWN SAUCE

Today's brown sauce is even simpler than velouté. Brown veal or beef stock\* is brought to the boil, then thickened by adding arrowroot\* or potato starch, which has been mixed to a thin paste with cold liquid, usually Madeira or water. The hot sauce thickens instantly with the paste, so add just enough to give the required consistency. Tomato purée may be added for colour, then the sauce is seasoned and simmered 5 or 10 minutes.

Nothing could be simpler, but in order for the sauce to be perfect, the stock used to make it must be very concentrated in flavour and rich with the gelatine from veal bones. If brown sauce lacks body, you can simmer it to concentrate the flavours, but take care, as arrowroot and potato starch lack the holding power of flour and sometimes go thin if overcooked.

A brown sauce which is too concentrated, with an almost bitter taste, can easily be remedied by adding a little stock or water.

Brown sauce is never served plain, but always developed by whisking in a little cold butter or adding flavouring such as wine, onions, shallots, mustard and herbs. Often these ingredients are combined and reduced to a concentrated essence before adding to the sauce. For example, bistro-style sauce piquante is flavoured with vinegar, shallots and

pickles and served with pork chops; sauce bercy, often served with roast beef and steak, has a reduction of white wine and shallots.

---

# WHITE SAUCE

## SAUCE BECHAMEL

When white sauce is served alone, the milk is usually infused with seasonings, but when a strong flavouring such as cheese is added this step may be omitted.

---

### MAKES ABOUT 8 fl oz/250ml SAUCE OF MEDIUM CONSISTENCY

| | |
|---|---|
| *8 fl oz/250 ml milk* | *¾ oz/20 g butter* |
| *slice of onion* | *1½ tablespoons flour* |
| *small bay leaf* | *salt and pepper* |
| *6 peppercorns* | *grated nutmeg* |

---

In a saucepan scald milk with onion, bay leaf and peppercorns, bringing it almost to the boil. Remove from heat, cover and let stand for 5-10 minutes to infuse.

Melt butter in a medium saucepan. Stir in flour with a whisk and cook over low heat 1-2 minutes until foaming but not browned.

Take pan from heat and strain in milk, whisking constantly. Return pan to heat and continue whisking until the sauce comes to the boil and thickens. Season with salt, pepper and nutmeg and simmer 2-3 minutes.

### GETTING AHEAD

While sauce is still hot, rub surface with a lump of butter to prevent a skin forming. White sauce can be kept uncovered at room temperature for 1-2 hours, or covered in the refrigerator for 2-3 days.

### VARIATIONS

*Thin White Sauce* (Sauce béchamel fluide)
Use only ½ oz/15 g butter and 1 tablespoon flour.
*Thick White Sauce* (Sauce béchamel épaisse)
Use 1 oz/25 g butter and 2 tablespoons flour.

*Cheese Sauce* (Sauce mornay)
Make 8 fl oz/250 ml thin white sauce, scalding milk but not infusing it with flavourings. Take sauce from heat and whisk in 1 egg yolk and ¾ oz/20 g grated Parmesan or Gruyère cheese. Stir until cheese has melted and taste.

**Note:** Do not reheat sauce or the cheese will cook into strings. Serve with eggs, poultry, fish and vegetables.

*Cream Sauce* (Sauce crème)
To 8 fl oz/250 ml medium white sauce add 2 fl oz/50 ml crème fraîche* or double cream. Simmer, whisking constantly, 1-2 minutes and taste. Serve with eggs, fish, vegetables and poultry.

*Mushroom Sauce* (Sauce aux champignons)
In a small saucepan put 2 oz/50 g thinly sliced mushrooms with 1-2 tablespoons water, a squeeze of lemon juice, salt and pepper. Press a piece of foil on top, cover with a lid and cook very gently until mushrooms are tender, 3-4 minutes. Stir mushrooms and liquid into 8 fl oz/250 ml thick white sauce, bring just to the boil and taste. Serve with fish, poultry and veal.

*Tomato Sauce* (Sauce aurore)
Make 8 fl oz/250 ml thin white sauce, scalding but not infusing the milk. Whisk in 2-3 teaspoons tomato purée and taste. Serve with eggs, fish, veal and poultry.

# VELOUTE SAUCE

## SAUCE VELOUTEE

Taste velouté often during simmering as seasoning is important.

---

### MAKES ABOUT 8fl oz/250 ml VELOUTE

| | |
|---|---|
| ½ pt/300ml well flavoured veal, chicken or fish stock* | 2 fl oz/50ml crème fraîche* or double cream (optional) |
| ¾ oz/20 g butter | squeeze of lemon juice (optional) |
| 1½ tablespoons flour | |
| salt and pepper | |

---

Bring stock to the boil.

Melt butter in a medium saucepan. Stir in flour with a whisk and cook 1-2 minutes until foaming but not browned.

Take pan from heat and whisk in stock. Return to heat and continue whisking until sauce comes to the boil and thickens. Season lightly as flavour will be concentrated during later cooking. Simmer sauce to required consistency, at least 10 minutes or up to 45 minutes. Whisk it occasionally.

Pour in cream, if using, and bring back to the boil. Strain sauce and taste. If bland, season it with lemon juice as well as salt and pepper.

### GETTING AHEAD

While sauce is still hot, rub surface with a lump of butter to prevent a skin forming. Velouté can be kept uncovered at room temperature for up to an hour, or covered in the refrigerator for 1-2 days.

### VARIATIONS

*Cream Velouté Sauce* (Sauce suprême)
Make 8 fl oz/250ml velouté sauce with chicken stock and add 2 oz/50 g chopped mushrooms during simmering. Strain the sauce and whisk in 2 fl oz/50ml double cream or crème fraîche*. Continue simmering to required consistency. Flavour with lemon

juice and taste. Add 1-2 tablespoons cold butter, off the heat, and shake pan until butter melts and is incorporated. Serve with poultry.

*Lemon and Parsley Velouté Sauce* (Sauce poulette)
Off the heat, whisk 1 tablespoon butter and 1 tablespoon chopped parsley into 8 fl oz/250 ml velouté made with veal stock. Taste, seasoning with lemon juice and a little grated nutmeg. Serve with sweetbreads, brains and vegetables.

*Mushroom Velouté Sauce* (Sauce veloutée aux champignons)
In a small saucepan put 2 oz/50 g thinly sliced mushrooms with 1-2 tablespoons water, a squeeze of lemon juice, salt and pepper. Press a piece of foil on top, cover with a lid and cook very gently until they are tender, 3-4 minutes. Stir mushrooms and liquid into 8 fl oz/250 ml velouté sauce, simmer to required consistency and taste. Add 1 oz/25 g cold butter, off the heat, and shake pan until butter melts and is incorporated. Serve with fish, poultry, veal.

*Tomato Velouté Sauce* (Sauce veloutée aurore)
Whisk 2-3 teaspoons tomato purée into 8 fl oz/ 250 ml velouté sauce and taste. Serve with eggs, fish, veal and poultry.

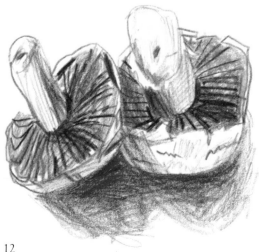

# BROWN SAUCE

## FOND DE VEAU LIE

The quickest of all basic sauces to make.

---

### MAKES ABOUT ¾ pt/450 ml
### BROWN SAUCE

| | |
|---|---|
| ¾ pt/450 ml brown veal stock* | 3 tablespoons Madeira or cold water |
| 1½ tablespoons arrowroot* or potato starch* | 1-2 teaspoons tomato purée (optional) |
| | salt and pepper |

---

Bring stock to the boil. In a cup mix arrowroot* or potato starch with Madeira or water to a thin paste.

Whisk paste into the boiling stock – it will thicken at once. Add only enough paste to thicken the sauce to the required consistency. Whisk in tomato purée, if using, adding enough to colour sauce slightly.

Strain sauce and taste for seasoning.

### GETTING AHEAD
Brown Sauce can be refrigerated for up to 3 days, or it can be frozen for up to 6 months.

### VARIATIONS
*Devil Sauce* (Sauce diable)
Boil 4 fl oz/125 ml white wine, 4 fl oz/125 ml white wine vinegar, 2 finely chopped shallots and 2 teaspoons tomato purée until reduced by two thirds. Stir in ¾ pt/450 ml brown sauce and bring to the boil. Take from the heat, whisk in 2-3 teaspoons Dijon mustard and taste. Serve with roast or grilled meats and chicken.

*Madeira Sauce* (Sauce madère)
Simmer 3 tablespoons Madeira with ¾ pt/450 ml brown sauce for 8-10 minutes. Take from the heat and whisk in 2 tablespoons more Madeira. Add 1-2 tablespoons cold butter and shake pan until butter

melts and is incorporated. Taste. Serve with kidneys, sweetbreads, tongue, fillet of beef, veal and ham.

*Piquant Sauce* (Sauce piquante)
Boil 2 finely chopped shallots with 4 fl oz/125 ml white wine and 4 fl oz/125 ml white wine vinegar until nearly dry. Add ¾ pt/450 ml brown sauce and simmer 5 minutes. Stir in 2 tablespoons coarsely chopped pickled gherkins, 1 tablespoon chopped parsley and 2 teaspoons chopped tarragon or chervil. Heat briefly and taste. Serve with pork and boiled beef.

*Red Wine and Beef Marrow Brown Sauce* (Sauce bordelaise)
Boil 8 fl oz/250 ml red wine with 2 finely chopped shallots until reduced by half. Stir in ¾ pt/450 ml brown sauce with ¼ teaspoon ground black pepper, bring to the boil and strain. Off the heat, add 1-2 tablespoons cold butter and shake pan until butter melts and is incorporated. Scoop marrow from 2 bones with a hot knife, slice and poach marrow 1-2 minutes in hot water. Drain. Add marrow to sauce and taste.

*Tomato Brown Sauce* (Sauce bretonne)
Sauté finely chopped onion in a little butter until soft but not browned. Add 8 fl oz/250 ml white wine and boil until reduced by half. Stir in ¾ pt/450 ml brown sauce, 2 tablespoons tomato purée and 1 crushed garlic clove. Simmer 10-15 minutes. Take from the heat, add 1-2 tablespoons cold butter and 1 tablespoon chopped parsley. Shake pan until butter melts and is incorporated. Taste. Serve with roast lamb, particularly when accompanied by dried white beans.

*Truffle Sauce* (Sauce Périgueux)
Simmer ¾ pt/450 ml brown sauce with 3 tablespoons Madeira and the juice from 1 small can truffles for 8-10 minutes. Take from heat and whisk in the diced truffles. Add 1-2 tablespoons cold butter and shake pan until butter melts and is incorporated. Serve with fillet of beef, ham and veal.

*White Wine and Mushroom Brown Sauce* (Sauce chasseur)
Sauté 2 finely chopped shallots in 1 tablespoon butter until soft but not browned. Add 2 oz/50 g thinly sliced mushrooms and cook until soft. Add 8 fl oz/250 ml white wine. Stir in ¾ pt/450 ml brown sauce and 2 tablespoons tomato purée and simmer 5 minutes. Take from the heat, add 1-2 tablespoons cold butter and 1 tablespoon chopped parsley. Shake pan until butter melts and is incorporated. Taste. Serve with all meats, roast chicken and rabbit.

*White Wine and Shallot Brown Sauce* (Sauce bercy)
Boil 4 fl oz/125 ml white wine with 2 finely chopped shallots until almost dry. Stir in ¾ pt/450 ml brown sauce, bring to the boil and taste. Serve with steak.

# 2
# EMULSIFIED SAUCES

The three emulsified sauces, mayonnaise, hollandaise and béarnaise, must be the most popular of all, yet they have only been known for a couple of hundred years. Legend has it that 'mahonnaise', now mayonnaise, was invented during the siege of Port Mahón at the end of the eighteenth century, when only eggs and oil were available to the governor's cook. Hollandaise and béarnaise are even younger, dating from the early nineteenth century. Certainly they are not obvious combinations, for they are tricky mixtures of oil or butter suspended in egg yolk. They have a reputation for caprice, for separating without warning, but given the right treatment they are as stable as any flour-based sauce.

## MAYONNAISE

The temperature of the ingredients is the key to making mayonnaise – they should be at room temperature or slightly warmer. (A chilled bowl of eggs straight from the refrigerator will prevent the mayonnaise thickening.) An emulsion must be established right at the start by whisking the egg yolks with salt, pepper, mustard and a little vinegar until thick. Then about a tablespoon of oil is added, drop by drop, whisking constantly so the mixture thickens further.

Once this emulsion has been established, the rest of the oil can be added quite fast in a steady stream. In fact I've seen professionals add all the remaining oil to mayonnaise in one carefree gesture, clocking a record-breaking time of 50 seconds from start to finish. Such speeds are easy to

equal with an electric mixer, but be sure to use a small bowl so the beaters catch hold of the yolks properly. In a blender or food processor you may need to double the quantity so the blades are in contact with the yolks.

If the mayonnaise remains persistently thin, this is a sign of curdling. Stop adding oil at once and whisk in a few drops of boiling water until the emulsion thickens. If this does not do the trick, an emulsion must be made again with a single egg yolk whisked with vinegar and seasonings. Beat in the curdled mixture as slowly as possible until a really thick emulsion is formed, then proceed as usual.

Proportions for mayonnaise are usually set at 1 egg yolk per ¼ pt/150 ml of oil. If too little oil is added, the mayonnaise will be thin and taste of egg; with too much oil it may start to separate. Flavours range from delicate, when vegetable oil is used, to nutty (walnut or hazelnut oil), to the pungent richness of virgin olive oil. Vinegar is the usual seasoning – the amount needed depends on its sharpness – but lemon juice is a favourite alternative along the Mediterranean, particularly with vegetables and fish.

At the end of mixing, mayonnaise will be thick enough to form peaks. This consistency is needed to bind salads such as potato, or vegetable macédoine. In country districts of France, a butter-yellow mound of mayonnaise is often served as accompaniment to shellfish, cold roast chicken or hard-boiled eggs. For coating, however, mayonnaise must be thinned with warm water, which also bleaches it to a paler cream colour. A tablespoon of water

is often enough to give the appropriate consistency, thickly coating the back of a spoon.

Given its popularity, it would seem sensible to make mayonnaise in large quantities, but unfortunately it cannot be kept for long. One day in a cool place is a maximum; one reason why bottled mayonnaise never tastes like homemade is that preservatives and stabilizers have been added. Storage time can be extended to 5 days in the refrigerator, but at this low temperature mayonnaise is liable to separate and it must be brought back fully to room temperature before it is stirred.

## HOLLANDAISE AND BEARNAISE

Hollandaise and béarnaise are hot, or more accurately warm, emulsified sauces based on egg yolks and melted butter. Proportions are standard – 2 oz/50 g of butter to each yolk so the sauce tastes neither too eggy nor too rich. For hollandaise, lemon juice is the standard flavouring, whilst béarnaise is bolstered with a pungent reduction of vinegar, white wine, peppercorns, shallots and tarragon. Because of its concentrated flavour, béarnaise is traditionally cooked until thick enough to hold a shape. It is served with red meats like beef and lamb, or fish such as salmon. The more delicate flavour of hollandaise demands a lighter texture, just coating a spoon, to serve with white fish and vegetables.

For both sauces, egg yolks are whisked over the heat to make a thick mousse, together with (for béarnaise) reduced vinegar or shallots or (for hollandaise) a tablespoon of water per egg yolk. Whisking should take 2 or 3 minutes and is one of the few occasions when a copper saucepan, preferably with sloping sides, is almost indispensable. A hollandaise mousse is done when it holds a ribbon trail for 30 seconds, but for béarnaise it should be thicker, stiff enough for the whisk to leave a clear trail across the base of the pan.

Melted butter is added to the mousse off the heat, a few drops at a time at first, and then in a steady stream once the sauce has formed an emulsion. Hollandaise or béarnaise rarely curdle at this stage, but if they seem thin as the butter is being added they may be too hot. Try whisking in an ice cube. Just occasionally a sauce is too thin because it is too cool: return the pan to the heat and cook a little longer.

Hollandaise and béarnaise can be kept in a bath of warm water for an hour or so, but here curdling is a real danger as the sauce must never be more than warm to the touch. Nor can it be reheated without likelihood of separation. If the worst does happen (invariably just as dinner is about to be served!) both sauces can be saved following the principles for mayonnaise. Whisk a fresh egg yolk and a tablespoon of water to a mousse, then add the curdled sauce.

## WHITE BUTTER SAUCE

Mayonnaise, béarnaise and hollandaise are not the only emulsified sauces, although they are the best known. White butter sauce, which is an emulsion of butter with a reduction of white wine vinegar, white wine and shallots, has recently become popular, particularly with fish. Lacking the stabilizer of egg yolk, white butter sauce is even more delicate than hollandaise. It must be made at the last moment, by whisking chilled pieces of butter into the warm shallot mixture. Heat should be just sufficient to melt the butter to creamy consistency without turning it to oil.

# MAYONNAISE

## SAUCE MAYONNAISE

Mayonnaise can be served plain, or with any of the flavourings suggested below. For a grand buffet, a trio of green, tomato and chantilly mayonnaise makes a colourful accompaniment to a whole poached fish.

---

## MAKES ABOUT ½ pt/300 ml MAYONNAISE

*2 egg yolks*

*salt and white pepper*

*2 tablespoons white wine vinegar or 1 tablespoon lemon juice, more if needed*

*pinch of dry mustard or 1 teaspoon Dijon mustard (optional)*

*½ pt/300 ml oil*

---

In a small bowl beat egg yolks with a little salt, pepper, half the vinegar or lemon juice and mustard, if using, until thick.

Add oil, drop by drop, whisking constantly. When about 2 tablespoons of oil have been added, the mixture should be very thick. If oil is added too quickly at this stage, mayonnaise will curdle.

Add remaining oil more quickly, a tablespoon at

a time, beating thoroughly between each addition. If using an electric beater, add the oil in a thin stream.

Stir in remaining vinegar or lemon juice, more mustard, salt and pepper to taste. The seasoning needed depends very much on the type of oil and vinegar used.

## GETTING AHEAD

To avoid curdling, mayonnaise is best stored at room temperature in a covered container. If refrigerated, it should be brought to room temperature before it is stirred. It can be kept 24 hours at room temperature, or up to 5 days if chilled. To prevent a film forming, press a wax paper directly on the surface.

## VARIATIONS

*Chantilly Mayonnaise*
To ½ pt/300 ml mayonnaise, fold in 2 fl oz/50 ml double cream, stiffly whipped, and taste for seasoning. Serve with vegetable salads.

*Garlic Mayonnaise* (Aïoli)
Omit the mustard. Pound 2 or 3 garlic cloves to a paste with ½ teaspoon coarse salt and mix thoroughly with the yolks and vinegar or lemon juice. Finish sauce using olive oil. Serve with vegetables, eggs and fish.

*Green Mayonnaise* (Mayonnaise verte)
Blanch* 4 oz/125 g spinach, watercress or parsley leaves (or a mixture of all three) in boiling salted water for 2 minutes. Drain, rinse with cold water and squeeze dry with your hands. Chop leaves very finely and stir into ½ pt/300 ml mayonnaise, or purée with mayonnaise in a blender or food processor. Taste for seasoning and serve with fish, eggs and vegetables.

*Rémoulade Sauce* (Sauce rémoulade)
To ½ pt/300 ml mayonnaise add 1 teaspoon Dijon mustard, 2 tablespoons chopped capers, 3 tablespoons chopped gherkin pickles, 2 tablespoons chopped parsley, 2 teaspoons tarragon and 1 teaspoon chopped anchovy fillets. Mix well, taste for seasoning, and serve with eggs, hot fried fish and cold meats.

*Tomato Mayonnaise* (Mayonnaise tomatée)
To ½ pt/300 ml mayonnaise add 1 or 2 tablespoons tomato purée and stir well.

# BEARNAISE SAUCE

## SAUCE BEARNAISE

Béarnaise is served with steak and grilled or sautéed fish such as salmon. For the best flavour, it is important to use fresh, not dried tarragon.

### MAKES 8 fl oz/250 ml

| | |
|---|---|
| 6 oz/175 g unsalted butter | 2 tablespoons chopped fresh tarragon stalks |
| 3 tablespoons white wine vinegar | 3 egg yolks |
| 3 tablespoons white wine | salt |
| 10 peppercorns, crushed | white or cayenne pepper |
| 3 shallots, finely chopped | 2 tablespoons finely chopped fresh tarragon leaves |

Melt butter, skim froth from surface, and let cool to tepid.

In a separate saucepan, boil vinegar and wine with peppercorns, chopped shallots and chopped tarragon stalks until reduced to 2 tablespoons. Allow to cool.

Whisk egg yolks, salt and pepper into shallot mixture and set pan over very low heat. Whisk constantly until mixture is mousse-like and thick enough to hold a ribbon trail when the whisk is lifted, at least 3 minutes. The base of the pan should never be more than hand-hot and if the mousse gets too hot it will separate.

Remove from heat and whisk in tepid butter, a little at a time, leaving buttermilk (white residue). When all butter has been added, work sauce through a fine strainer, pressing well to extract all the mixture. Alternatively, sauce can be left without straining so shallots and tarragon add texture.

Add finely chopped tarragon leaves and taste sauce for seasoning.

### GETTING AHEAD

Béarnaise is best served at once. However, it can be made up to an hour ahead and kept in a bath of warm, not hot, water. Stir it from time to time.

### VARIATIONS

*Tomato Béarnaise* (Sauce choron)

To 8 fl oz/250 ml béarnaise sauce add 1½ tablespoons tomato purée. Serve with steak, fish and eggs.

*Green Peppercorn Béarnaise* (Béarnaise au poivre vert)

Omit chopped tarragon leaves added at the end of béarnaise sauce and add 1 tablespoon drained and crushed green peppercorns to every cup of sauce. Serve with steak and salmon.

# HOLLANDAISE SAUCE

## SAUCE HOLLANDAISE

Hollandaise sauce is served with poached fish, vegetables and eggs.

---

### MAKES 8 fl oz/250 ml

| | |
|---|---|
| 6 oz/175 g unsalted butter | 3 egg yolks |
| 3 tablespoons water | salt and pepper |
| | juice of ½ lemon |

---

In a small saucepan, melt butter, skim froth from surface and allow to cool until tepid.

In a separate saucepan mix water and egg yolks with a little salt and pepper. Set over very low heat and whisk constantly until mixture is mousse-like and thick enough for the whisk to leave a trail on bottom of the pan. It will take at least 3 minutes. Do not allow the base of the pan to become more than hand-hot because if the mousse gets too hot it will separate.

Remove pan from heat and gradually whisk in tepid butter, a little at a time, leaving the buttermilk (white residue) at bottom of the pan. Stir in lemon juice and taste for seasoning.

### GETTING AHEAD

Hollandaise is best served at once but it can be made up to an hour ahead and kept in a bath of warm, not hot, water. Stir the sauce from time to time.

### VARIATIONS

*Chantilly Sauce* (Sauce chantilly)
To 8 fl oz/250 ml hollandaise sauce, add 2 fl oz/50 ml double cream, stiffly whipped, and taste for seasoning. Serve with fish, chicken, sautéed sweetbreads and asparagus.

*Mustard Sauce* (Sauce moutarde)
To 8 fl oz/250 ml hollandaise sauce, add 1-2 teaspoons Dijon mustard to taste. Serve with eggs and fish.

# WHITE BUTTER SAUCE

## BEURRE BLANC

White butter sauce comes from the Loire Valley and traditionally is made with the local Sancerre wine to serve with pike from the river. Based on any dry white wine it is a perfect accompaniment for all kinds of fish.

---

### MAKES ABOUT 8 fl oz/250 ml

| | |
|---|---|
| 3 tablespoons white wine vinegar | 2 finely chopped shallots |
| 3 tablespoons dry white wine | ½ lb/250 g cold unsalted butter, cut in small pieces |
| | salt and pepper |

---

In a small saucepan, boil wine vinegar, wine and shallots until reduced to 1 tablespoon.

Reduce heat and whisk in butter gradually, in small pieces, to make a smooth creamy sauce. Work sometimes over low heat and sometimes off the heat, so that the butter softens and thickens the sauce without melting enough to be oily.

Season and serve as soon as possible. If the sauce must be kept warm for a few minutes, set pan on a rack over warm but not boiling water.

# 3
# SALADS

For much of my life, along with most of the French, I regarded salad as tossed greens to be eaten after the main course to clean the palate before cheese. Alternatively, salad might appear as first course 'crudités' – a mixed group of vegetables such as grated carrot, marinated cucumber and tomato vinaigrette. Changes might be struck with a shellfish salad, or one of the tempting vegetable salads from Provence, aromatic with olive oil and herbs. But the imagination stopped there.

Recently, however, salads have blossomed on the French menu, appearing as a lively first course or sometimes even a main dish. They have come to include smoked fish, duck breast, chicken livers (or foie gras for the well heeled), with exotic fruits like mango and seasonings such as saffron or pink peppercorns. Cooks have been playing with temperature, adding hot sautéed mushrooms or liver to cold salad greens.

Combinations can be unexpected, but when they are successful they always follow the traditional rules for colour, taste and texture. First, colours should be in cheerful contrast to each other – tomato and olives with chicken, or carrots, peas and turnips in the classic macédoine. Second, tastes should marry agreeably, with a delicate dressing for greens and more potent flavours like mustard and pickles for meats and fish. Third, texture should be either crisp, chewy or tender, and not an unsatisfying combination of all three.

The type of oil and vinegar used with salads is obviously

vital. Nine times out of ten the French would choose red or white wine vinegar, finding malt or spirit vinegar too harsh. Alternatives are sherry vinegar or cider and fruit vinegars such as raspberry and blackcurrant. Along the Mediterranean the vinegar is often replaced by lemon juice – it makes a happy marriage in cold fish salads.

Olive oil is good with root vegetables, particularly potato, while nut oils are delicious in the occasional nouvelle cuisine 'salade folle' (p. 27) of salad greens combined with shellfish, foie gras or chicken liver, nuts and a slice or two of tropical fruit.

## VINAIGRETTE DRESSING

The term vinaigrette is a misnomer, for this dressing should never actually taste of vinegar. On the contrary, the flavour of vinaigrette should be a careful balance of its few ingredients – oil, vinegar, Dijon mustard, salt and pepper. Classic proportions (and they rarely vary) are three parts oil to one of vinegar. If lemon juice replaces vinegar, use proportions of four to one. The amount of mustard depends on its piquancy, but a teaspoon for every 4 tablespoons of dressing is typical.

Vinaigrette takes scarcely 2 minutes to make – 1 minute to assemble the ingredients and one to whisk them together. Vinegar, mustard, salt and pepper go together in a small bowl and are beaten for 10 seconds until mixed. The oil is added in a slow but steady stream, whisking constantly so the dressing thickens slightly to form an emulsion. The mustard is a help here and a spoonful or two

of cream may be substituted for some of the oil. The emulsion separates on standing, but can be quickly reformed with vigorous whisking. Do not leave dressing in contact with a metal whisk or aluminium bowl.

The standard vinaigrette is made with vegetable oil and wine vinegar, to which all sorts of flavourings may be added. Top choice is chopped fresh herbs such as parsley, basil, chives, tarragon or chervil; they should be whisked in just before use, otherwise they will discolour. Shallot, very finely chopped, is good with meats and root vegetables, together with capers and pickled gherkins if you like a piquant dressing, technically known as sauce ravigote. Garlic is used in vinaigrette less commonly than supposed, and then only in small quantities – a cut clove rubbed on the bowl can be sufficient to perfume a whole salad. Except very occasionally with fruit, the English habit of adding a pinch of sugar to vinaigrette is taboo.

## VINAIGRETTE SALADS

Most vinaigrette salads are so simple as to need no recipe: sliced fresh tomatoes in olive oil and lemon juice with a scattering of herbs, shallot and garlic; grated carrots mixed with oil and wine vinegar; boiled baby new potatoes, peeled and soaked in oil and white wine. In France, green salad is pure green, often consisting of only one kind of lettuce and a plain dressing.

As well as flavouring salad, vinaigrette also acts as a marinade. At least an hour or even up to a day of soaking in vinaigrette can be of great benefit to root vegetables and meats. A sliced mushroom salad or a vegetable macédoine simply does not taste the same unless marinated in dressing. However marinating is disastrous to lettuce, which must be tossed only at the last moment as it can wilt within 15 minutes.

To toss or not to toss is a matter for debate as vinaigrette can also be spooned over a salad after it has been arranged on individual plates. Tossed salad tastes better as ingredients are completely coated and flavours have a chance to blend. Seasoning can be checked after mixing so it is just right. However arranged salads look much prettier on the plate and, with the current emphasis on presentation, they have become almost the rule. A good deal depends on the ingredients – sliced tomatoes cannot be tossed in any case, and it is a shame to bury shrimps or foie gras in a mass of greens.

## MAYONNAISE SALADS

The other common dressing for salad, mayonnaise (p. 16), is less versatile than vinaigrette as it is so rich.

Mayonnaise is appropriate for fish, hard-boiled eggs, chicken, and salads of root vegetables. Both mayonnaise and vinaigrette may be called for in a recipe. The vinaigrette is added first, often to ingredients that are still hot so the dressing is absorbed easily. Then when the ingredients are cold, mayonnaise is mixed in to bind them.

Once mixed with mayonnaise, a salad sours quickly, particularly if it includes fish. Four or five hours in the refrigerator is the maximum storage time. Foods such as hard-boiled eggs, coated with mayonnaise can only be kept an hour or two because they develop a thin yellow film of oil, which is unsightly though harmless.

---

# VINAIGRETTE DRESSING

## SAUCE VINAIGRETTE

Add chopped herbs, shallot and a touch of garlic to your taste. For a ravigote sauce to serve with cold meats add chopped capers, pickled gherkins and a generous quantity of parsley as well.

---

### MAKES 2 fl oz/50 ml DRESSING

| | |
|---|---|
| 1 tablespoon vinegar **or** 2 teaspoons lemon juice | salt and pepper |
| 1 teaspoon Dijon mustard, or to taste | 3 tablespoons oil |

---

In a small bowl combine vinegar or lemon juice, mustard, salt and pepper. Whisk until thoroughly mixed and the salt is dissolved, about 20 seconds.

Add oil in a slow, steady stream, whisking constantly. The dressing should emulsify so it is the consistency of thin cream. Taste for seasoning.

### GETTING AHEAD

Vinaigrette dressing can be prepared up to a week in advance and stored in a screwtop jar. Keep it in a cool place. If chilled, the oil may solidify but will melt again as soon as it is brought to room temperature. Whisk dressing vigorously or shake in a jar to re-emulsify it before using.

# LETTUCE SALAD WITH CROUTES

## SALADE DE LAITUE AUX CHAPONS

Any lettuce can be used for this salad, though cos or curly endive are traditional.

### SERVES 4-6

| | |
|---|---|
| 1 lettuce (about ¾ lb/375 g) | 1 crusty roll or 4 thin slices French bread |
| 1 clove garlic, crushed | 4 fl oz/125 ml vinaigrette dressing made with 2 teaspoons mustard, lemon juice and olive oil (p. 22) |
| 1 oz/25 g butter, creamed | |
| salt and pepper | |

Wash lettuce thoroughly, tearing any large leaves into 2 or 3 pieces; dry well. Set oven at 175°C/350°F/gas 4. Line a baking sheet with foil.

Beat garlic into creamed butter with salt and pepper. Cut roll into ½ in/1.5 cm slices and spread with garlic butter. If using bread slices, spread with garlic butter and cut in quarters.

Set bread croûtes on baking sheet, buttered side up, and bake until browned, 15-20 minutes. Let cool. Make vinaigrette dressing.

Put lettuce in a salad bowl, add dressing and toss. Taste for seasoning. Add croûtes and toss again.

### GETTING AHEAD

Lettuce, croûtes, and dressing can be prepared 24 hours ahead. Keep lettuce, lightly wrapped in a tea towel, in the refrigerator. Store croûtes in airtight container. Toss salad just before serving.

### VARIATION

Caesar Salad (Salade César)
Add 4 finely chopped anchovy fillets and ¾ oz/20 g grated Parmesan cheese to dressing just before tossing the salad. When salad is tossed, break in a whole egg and toss thoroughly again. Finally add croûtes; toss again and serve.

# SPINACH SALAD WITH BACON AND VINEGAR

## SALADE D'EPINARDS AUX LARDONS ET AU VINAIGRE

In this popular variation of vinaigrette, oil is replaced by hot bacon fat and the pan juices are dissolved in vinegar. Hot dressings like this need robust greens, such as curly endive, chicory or spinach.

### SERVES 4

| | |
|---|---|
| 1 lb/500 g fresh spinach | 2 tablespoons vinegar |
| 2 hard-boiled eggs | salt and pepper |
| ¼ lb/125 g piece bacon | |

Discard spinach stalks and wash leaves thoroughly. Drain them and pat dry with paper. Put them in a salad bowl.

Separate egg whites from yolks. Coarsely chop whites and reserve; sieve yolks over the spinach.

Cut bacon into small cubes and sauté in a frying pan until crisp. Discard all but about 4 tablespoons fat. Pour fat with bacon over spinach and toss immediately; the heat will wilt the leaves slightly. Add vinegar to frying pan and heat gently, stirring to dissolve pan juices. Pour over salad and toss again. Add pepper, toss thoroughly and taste for seasoning; salt may not be needed. Sprinkle salad with chopped egg white and serve at once from the salad bowl.

### GETTING AHEAD

Spinach and chopped egg can be prepared up to 4 hours ahead and kept covered. Bacon must be fried and salad tossed at the last moment.

### VARIATION

Spinach Salad with Chicken Livers (Salade d'épinards aux foies de volaille)
Substitute 3 chicken livers for boiled eggs and bacon. Toss spinach with 4 tablespoons vinaigrette

made with olive oil and wine vinegar (p. 22). Cut chicken livers in 2-3 slices and sauté them in 1 tablespoon butter until brown but still very pink in the centre. It will take 1-2 minutes. Add 1 tablespoon vinegar and continue cooking ½ minute. Add livers and vinegar to salad, toss and taste for seasoning. Serve at once.

# PROVENÇALE PEPPER AND TOMATO SALAD

## SALADE DE POIVRONS ET TOMATES PROVENÇALE

If possible, use a mixture of red, green and yellow peppers for this salad.

### SERVES 4

| | |
|---|---|
| 4 tablespoons olive oil | 3 tomatoes, peeled, seeded and coarsely chopped* |
| 4 mixed red, green and yellow peppers, cored, seeded and cut in wide strips | 1 clove garlic, crushed |
| salt and pepper | 1 teaspoon thyme |
| 1 onion, thinly sliced | 1 tablespoon chopped parsley |

Heat 3 tablespoons oil in a sauté pan and add the peppers, salt and pepper. Cook over medium heat, stirring to coat peppers thoroughly with oil, 2-3 minutes. Cover and cook over low heat until peppers are almost tender, 8-10 minutes. Remove them.

Add remaining oil to pan and cook onion until soft. Add tomatoes, garlic, thyme, parsley, salt and pepper and simmer, stirring occasionally, 4-5 minutes. Return peppers and simmer 2-3 minutes longer. Let cool and taste for seasoning. Serve at room temperature.

### GETTING AHEAD

The salad can be made up to 3 days ahead and refrigerated, if you wish.

# RED CABBAGE SALAD WITH APPLES

## SALADE DE CHOU ROUGE AUX POMMES

This salad would normally form part of a first course selection of different salads, such as tomato, cucumber, grated carrot or green bean salad.

### SERVES 6

| | |
|---|---|
| 1 small red cabbage (about 1 lb/500 g) | 4 fl oz/125 ml vinaigrette dressing made with lemon juice and vegetable oil (p. 22) |
| 4 tablespoons red wine vinegar | |
| | 1-2 firm eating apples |

Cut cabbage in quarters and discard the core. Very finely shred the leaves with a sharp knife, mandoline slicer or food processor. Bring vinegar to the boil, pour over cabbage and toss well. The cabbage will turn bright red.

Make dressing; peel, quarter and core apples. Cut them in matchsticks and add to dressing at once to prevent them from discolouring. Toss well.

Mix cabbage with apples and dressing, taste and pile salad in a bowl. Chill before serving.

### GETTING AHEAD

Salad can be made up to 8 hours ahead and refrigerated, if you wish.

### VARIATION

*Red Cabbage Salad with Apples and Roquefort* (Salade de chou rouge aux pommes et roquefort)

Cut 2-3 crusty bread rolls in ½ in/1 cm slices. To make croûtes* bake bread in a 175°C/350°F/gas 4 oven until crisp and golden, 10-15 minutes. With a fork crush 3 oz/75 g Roquefort cheese and work in 1-2 tablespoons milk to make a paste. Spread paste on croûtes. Pile red cabbage and apple salad on individual plates and set cheese croûtes around the edge. Serve as a light main course.

# SALAD OF COOKED VEGETABLES

## MACEDOINE DE LEGUMES

Various vegetables can be used in a macédoine, but it should always contain carrots and green beans or peas for colour, as well as a white root vegetable such as turnip, parsnip or celeriac. Cooked vegetable salad is good with cold meats, fish or chicken.

---

### SERVES 4

½ lb/250 g diced carrot

½ lb/250 g diced turnip, parsnip or celeriac

6 oz/175 g shelled peas

6 oz/175 g green beans, cut in ½ in/1 cm lengths

2 fl oz/50 ml vinaigrette dressing made with white wine or malt vinegar and olive oil (p. 22)

6 fl oz/175 ml mayonnaise (p. 16)

---

Put carrot and turnip, parsnip or celeriac in cold salted water, cover and bring to the boil. Simmer until just tender, 10-12 minutes, and drain.

Cook peas and green beans separately in boiling salted water until tender but still firm, 5-8 minutes. Drain, rinse with cold water and drain thoroughly again.

Mix vinaigrette with vegetables while they are still warm.

When cold, stir vegetables with enough mayonnaise to bind them lightly; if too much is added the salad will be heavy. Taste for seasoning.

### GETTING AHEAD
Cooked vegetable salad improves in flavour if it is made at least 1 and up to 4 hours ahead. Keep it covered in the refrigerator.

### VARIATION
*Stuffed Tomatoes with Cooked Vegetable Salad* (Tomates farcies à la macédoine de légumes)
For a first course for eight, core 8 large ripe tomatoes and cut a slice from the cored end so they sit flat. Make two parallel vertical cuts (½ in/1 cm apart) to halfway down the tomato and remove 2 wedges from the sides, leaving a handle in the middle. Scoop out the seeds with a teaspoon and sprinkle the insides of the tomatoes with salt. Turn upside down to drain for 15 minutes. Fill with cooked vegetable salad and chill before serving.

# MUSSEL AND POTATO SALAD

## SALADE DIEPPOISE

The town of Dieppe, on the English Channel, is famous for its tiny, piquant mussels.

### SERVES 4

| | |
|---|---|
| 1 lb/500 g small firm potatoes | 6 fl oz/175 ml mayonnaise (p. 16) |
| salt and pepper | 4 lb/2 kg mussels, cleaned, cooked and shelled* |
| 2 fl oz/50 ml vinaigrette dressing made with white wine vinegar and olive oil (p. 22) | 5-6 stalks celery, very finely diced, with their leaves |

Put potatoes, unpeeled, in cold salted water, cover and bring to the boil. Simmer until just tender, 15-20 minutes. Drain.

Peel potatoes while still warm, cut in ½ in/1 cm slices and mix gently with vinaigrette. When warm, the potatoes will absorb the dressing better.

When potatoes are cool, stir in mayonnaise with mussels and celery. Taste for seasoning. Pile salad in a bowl and decorate with celery tops.

### GETTING AHEAD

Potatoes in vinaigrette, mussels and mayonnaise can be prepared separately up to 6 hours ahead and refrigerated. Mix them an hour or two before serving so the flavours mellow.

### VARIATION

Mussel and Pasta Salad (Salade de moules à l'italienne)

Substitute ½ lb/250 g macaroni or shell pasta for the potatoes. Cook pasta in boiling salted water until tender but still firm; cooking time depends on size of pasta. Drain, rinse with hot water and drain thoroughly. Toss while still hot with vinaigrette dressing, and finish as mussel and potato salad.

# CHICKEN SALAD WITH TOMATOES AND OLIVES

## SALADE DE POULET NIÇOISE

If possible, use the little black Nice olives for this recipe, which is good for leftover cooked chicken.

### SERVES 4

| | |
|---|---|
| 4 lb/2 kg chicken, cooked, or 4 pieces cooked chicken | 2 tablespoons chopped fresh basil or oregano or 1 tablespoon chopped fresh chives |
| 1-2 tablespoons tomato purée | |
| 6 fl oz/175 ml mayonnaise (p. 16) | 2 fl oz/50 ml vinaigrette dressing made with lemon juice and olive oil (p. 22) |
| paprika (for sprinkling) | |
| 3-4 large tomatoes, peeled* | 4 oz/125 g black olives |

Cut the whole chicken in 4 pieces*; discard skin from chicken.

Stir enough tomato purée into mayonnaise to colour and flavour it.

To assemble salad: set a piece of chicken on one side of four individual plates. Coat chicken with mayonnaise, reserving the rest to serve separately. Sprinkle chicken lightly with paprika. Slice tomatoes and arrange, overlapping, on other side of plates. Add herbs to vinaigrette dressing and spoon over tomatoes. Pile olives in centre of plates. Serve salad at room temperature.

### GETTING AHEAD

Chicken, mayonnaise, vinaigrette and tomatoes can be prepared separately 6-8 hours ahead and refrigerated. Assemble salad not more than 1 hour before serving.

### VARIATION

Make a fish salad by substituting cooked fish steaks, such as cod or sea bass, for the chicken.

# CRAZY SALAD

## SALADE FOLLE

Create your own 'crazy' combinations, substituting meats, fish or poultry for the chicken livers.

### SERVES 6

| | |
|---|---|
| 1 stalk celery, very thinly sliced | 2 tablespoons vegetable oil |
| ½ lb/250 g leaf lettuce or lamb's lettuce | 1 shallot, finely chopped |
| 2 oz/50 g pine nuts **or** coarsely chopped walnuts | 4 fl oz/125 ml walnut oil |
| 1 mango **or** 2 oranges | 3 tablespoons fruit vinegar or wine vinegar |
| ¼ lb/125 g cooked small prawns/shrimps | 4 chicken livers, cut in 3-4 slices |
| | salt and pepper |

Soak celery slices in iced water to crisp them.

Wash and dry salad greens. Tear large leaves in 2-3 pieces and put in a large salad bowl with pine nuts or walnuts. Peel and slice mango. If using oranges, cut away skin and pith with a serrated knife. Separate sections, discarding membrane and add to salad greens. Drain celery, dry and add to bowl with prawns.

In sauté pan, heat half the vegetable oil, add shallot and cook until soft, 2-3 minutes. Pour hot shallots and oil over salad and toss. Add walnut oil with half the vinegar, season and toss.

Sprinkle chicken livers with salt and pepper and sauté in remaining vegetable oil for 1-2 minutes. Livers should be brown but still pink in the centre. Add vinegar to hot sauté pan and shake to dissolve juices. Pile salad on individual plates and spoon livers on top. Serve at once while still hot.

### GETTING AHEAD
Salad greens, fruit and celery can be prepared several hours in advance. Sauté chicken livers and toss salad with vinegar and oil just before serving.

# HAM, POTATO AND PEPPER SALAD

## SALADE BAYONNAISE

Bayonne in the Pyrenees is famous for its ham.

### SERVES 6

| | |
|---|---|
| 3 lb/1.5 kg firm potatoes | 1 red pepper, cored, seeded and diced |
| salt and pepper | ½ lb/250 g cooked ham, diced |
| 2 fl oz/50 ml white wine | 6 fl oz/175 ml mayonnaise (p. 16) |
| 2 fl oz/50 ml white wine vinegar | 4 oz/125 g black olives |
| 1 green pepper, cored, seeded and diced | |

Put potatoes, unpeeled, in cold salted water, cover and bring to the boil. Simmer until just tender, 15-20 minutes, and drain. Peel while still warm, cut them into chunks and sprinkle with white wine, vinegar, salt and pepper. Potatoes will absorb seasonings best when warm.

Cook red and green peppers in boiling salted water until tender but still firm, 1-2 minutes. Drain, rinse with cold water and drain thoroughly.

Mix cool potatoes with peppers, ham and mayonnaise. Taste for seasoning, pile in a serving bowl on individual plates and decorate with olives.

### GETTING AHEAD
Salad should be prepared at least 1 hour and up to 4 hours ahead so the flavours mellow. Keep it in the refrigerator.

### VARIATION
*Salt Cod, Potato and Pepper Salad* (Salade basquaise) Omit ham. Soak 1 lb/500 g salt cod overnight in cold water. Drain, put in a saucepan and add milk to cover. Cover with lid and simmer until fish flakes easily, 10-15 minutes. Drain and flake, discarding bones and skin. Add to salad instead of ham.

27

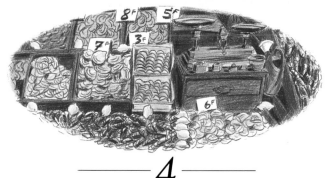

# 4
# SAUTES

A sauté calls for judgement and a watchful eye on the stove. The first step is the process of sautéing itself – from the French verb 'sauter', to jump. The term implies frying pieces of meat or vegetables in a pan over a high heat in a small amount of butter or fat – they will splutter and jump as they brown lightly. Then the heat is reduced and the sauté is covered and left to simmer gently in its own juices, thus developing a delicious buttery taste. A little wine or stock may be added at this stage to deglaze the pan.

In a sauté, the garnish and flavourings are added when the main ingredient is half or almost completely cooked. Flavourings may include herbs, spices, vegetables and even shellfish or dried fruits. A sauté is one of the most versatile of all dishes; for chicken alone, literally hundreds of variations are listed in classic cookbooks. More than once I've made up my own, adding the glass of wine, the mushroom or carrot, the tomato or two, that I happen to have in the refrigerator. Cooking time for a sauté is relatively short, an hour at most, so the garnish retains its distinctive flavour, as should the main ingredient itself. There is little of the blending and mellowing found in a good ragoût.

Under these cooking conditions, tender cuts are vital, making a sauté a more expensive, semi-luxury dish. Poultry (chicken, duck, guinea fowl) is particularly suitable, as are game birds like pigeon and pheasant. Veal, rabbit, offal like kidneys, and firm-fleshed fish and shellfish are all good, too, but beef and lamb are rarely used as only chops or steak cook quickly enough. No matter what the meat, it is important that all pieces should be cut the same size and be in contact with the bottom of the pan so that they cook evenly.

A sauté must never be drowned in a liquid. On the contrary, it must be allowed to evaporate, lid off or half off, so the sauce gently simmers and reduces. It must not, however, catch on the bottom of the pan – hence the need for a watchful eye. At the end of cooking, only 2 or 3 tablespoons of sauce per person should remain, the concentrated essence of all the different ingredients. Sautés are normally cooked on top of the stove, after the initial browning, though in a moderate oven, 180°C/ 350°F/gas 4 they require less attention. A deep frying pan or shallow casserole can be used to make a sauté, but it is worth investing in a proper sauté pan which has a wide, heavy base and 3-4 in/7-10 cm sides to control evaporation of liquid. The handle should be heatproof in case you want to put the pan in the oven, and the lid should fit neatly but not so tightly that some steam cannot escape.

Like any dish cooked in a sauce, a sauté reheats well, though this must be done carefully so the ingredients do not stick. Rice or noodles are a good accompaniment to recipes like sauté of chicken with mussels and veal escalopes sautéed with port and with any sauté, I have a partiality for small fried potatoes. Nothing else is needed as the recipe normally includes a variety of vegetables.

# Saute of Monkfish with Basil and Fennel

## SAUTE DE LOTTE AU BASILIC ET FENOUIL

Monkfish has a firm flesh which makes it the ideal fish for a sauté.

### SERVES 6

| | |
|---|---|
| 3 bulbs fennel (about 3 lb/1.5 kg) | 6 fl oz/175 ml white wine |
| 4 lb/2 kg monkfish, with the bone | 1 oz/25 g chopped fresh basil |
| 1 oz/25 g butter | 1 oz/25 g chopped fresh chives |
| salt and pepper | |
| 8 fl oz/250 ml crème fraîche* or double cream | 3 tomatoes, peeled, seeded and coarsely chopped* |

Trim top and root from fennel and cut bulbs in half. Discard core, which can be bitter. Cook fennel in boiling salted water until almost tender, 10-15 minutes. Drain and slice fennel in thin strips.

Cut backbone from monkfish and trim flesh of all dark skin and transparent membrane. Cut flesh into finger-sized strips.

Heat butter in sauté pan and add fennel. Sprinkle with salt and pepper and sauté until fennel is very lightly browned, 2-3 minutes. Remove it.

Sprinkle fish with salt and pepper. Add to sauté pan and cook, tossing occasionally, until firm and white, 4-5 minutes; do not allow it to brown. Keep warm with the fennel.

Add wine to pan and stir to dissolve pan juices. Boil until reduced by half. Stir in cream, bring to boil and strain into a saucepan. Add basil and half the chives and replace monkfish and fennel. Mix well and taste sauce for seasoning. Cover and keep warm over low heat so flavours mellow 3-5 minutes.

To serve: arrange fish and fennel on individual plates. Sprinkle with tomatoes and remaining chives.

### GETTING AHEAD
Fennel, fish and herbs can be prepared 6-8 hours ahead. Sauté them in butter and complete the dish just before serving.

### VARIATION
*Sauté of Squid with Basil and Fennel* (Sauté d'encornets au basilic et fenouil)
Substitute 2 lb/1 kg squid for the monkfish. Clean squid and discard the spine, eyes and any black skin. Cut tentacles from body and chop in pieces; slice the body. Sauté squid in butter as for monkfish. Add wine, cover and simmer until tender, 20-25 minutes. If necessary remove lid at end of cooking so wine evaporates by half. Remove squid, add cream and finish as for monkfish.

# Saute of Chicken with Tomato

## SAUTE DE POULET PORTUGAISE

One of the simplest of all sautés.

### SERVES 4

| | |
|---|---|
| 3 lb/1.5kg chicken, cut into 8 pieces* | 2 shallots, finely chopped |
| salt and pepper | 2 cloves garlic, crushed |
| 1 tablespoon oil | 3 large tomatoes, peeled, seeded and chopped* or 1 14 oz/400 g can chopped tomatoes |
| ½ oz/15 g butter | |
| 2 onions, sliced | 2 teaspoons tomato purée |
| 4 fl oz/125 ml white wine | bouquet garni* |
| 4 fl oz/125 ml chicken stock*, more if needed | fried croûtes* |

Season chicken pieces with salt and pepper.
In sauté pan heat oil and butter until foaming.

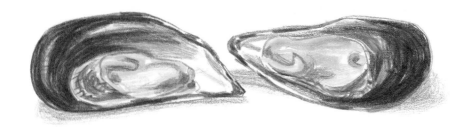

Add chicken and brown over medium heat, turning from time to time, about 15 minutes.

Remove chicken from pan and add onions. Cook over a low heat until golden, 5-7 minutes. Stir in white wine, stock, shallots, garlic, tomatoes, tomato purée, bouquet garni and salt and pepper. Return chicken and bring just to the boil.

Cover and simmer over low heat, stirring occasionally, until the chicken is tender, 15-20 minutes. Add more stock during cooking if the sauce gets dry. If breast pieces are done before legs, remove and keep warm.

Make croûtes.

To finish: taste sauce for seasoning. Transfer chicken pieces to a serving dish or to individual plates and spoon sauce over them. Decorate with croûtes and serve.

### GETTING AHEAD

The chicken can be cooked up to 48 hours ahead. Reheat on top of the stove or in a 180°C/350°F/gas 4 oven. Prepare croûtes just before serving.

### VARIATION

*Sautéed Veal Escalopes with Tomato* (Escalopes de veau sautées portugaise)
Substitute 4 veal escalopes for chicken. Season escalopes with salt and pepper and coat with flour, patting meat to discard excess flour. Sauté escalopes in oil and butter until brown, 1-2 minutes on each side. Remove them, make onion and tomato mixture, and simmer 10 minutes. Return escalopes to pan and simmer in mixture until tender when pierced with a two pronged fork, 4-5 minutes.

# SAUTE OF CHICKEN WITH MUSSELS

## SAUTE DE POULET AUX MOULES

The chicken in this recipe is pickled overnight in salt before cooking, giving it a piquant flavour.

### SERVES 4

| | |
|---|---|
| 3 lb/1.5 kg chicken cut into 8 pieces* | 1 tablespoon chopped parsley |
| 1 oz/25 g rock salt | **For sauce** |
| 1 oz/25 g flour | ¼ lb/125 g mushrooms |
| salt and pepper | 4 fl oz/125 ml crème fraîche* or double cream |
| 1 tablespoon oil | |
| ½ oz/15 g butter | juice of ½ lemon |
| ½ pt/300 ml chicken stock*, more if necessary | grated nutmeg |
| 2½ lb/1.25 kg mussels, cleaned, cooked and shelled* | 2 cloves garlic, finely chopped |
| | 1½ oz/40 g butter |

Rub pieces of chicken with rock salt, pack in a small bowl (not aluminium), cover and refrigerate 12-18 hours.

Wipe all salt from chicken and pat dry with paper towels. Season flour with salt and pepper and coat chicken with it, patting off excess.

In the sauté pan heat oil and butter until foaming. Add chicken pieces and brown them over medium heat, turning from time to time, about 15 minutes.

In a small saucepan boil stock until reduced by half. Add to browned chicken, cover and cook over low heat until chicken is tender, 15-20 minutes. If pan gets dry, add more stock. If breast pieces are done before legs, remove them and keep warm.

For the sauce: in a food processor or blender purée mushrooms with the cream. Season to taste with lemon juice, nutmeg and pepper; salt may not be needed as mussels are salty.

To finish: take chicken from pan and keep warm. Add cream mixture to pan with garlic and bring to the boil, stirring to dissolve pan juices. Strain and skim off any fat. Return chicken to sauce and add mussels. Heat gently for 5 minutes so flavours blend. Taste for seasoning.

Add butter in small pieces, shaking pan to mix them into the sauce. Transfer chicken to a serving dish or individual plates, spoon mussels and sauce over it, sprinkle with parsley and serve.

### GETTING AHEAD
Chicken, mussels and sauce can be prepared separately up to 12 hours ahead. Combine them and finish the dish just before serving.

### VARIATION
*Sauté of Chicken with Curry (Sauté de poulet indienne)*
Substitute ¾ lb/375 kg cooked, peeled medium prawns/shrimps for the shelled mussels and omit the mushrooms. When chicken is brown, add 1 tablespoon curry powder, or to taste, to the pan and sauté 1 minute. Add stock and finish as for chicken with mussels.

# SAUTE OF DUCK WITH DRIED FRUITS

## SAUTE DE CANARD AGENAISE

Agen, in south-western France, is a centre for drying fruits, particularly prunes.

---

### SERVES 4

| | |
|---|---|
| 4-5 lb/2-2.5 kg duck, cut into 6 pieces* | ¼ lb/125 g dried pitted prunes |
| salt and pepper | ¾ pt/450 ml chicken or veal stock*, more if necessary |
| 1 tablespoon oil | |
| 2 oz/50 g butter | |
| ¼ lb/125 g dried apple rings | juice of ½ lemon |
| | 2½ oz/65 g slivered almonds, toasted |
| ¼ lb/125 g dried apricots | |

---

Season duck pieces with salt and pepper.

Heat oil in sauté pan with ½ oz/15 g of the butter until foaming. Add pieces of duck, skin side down and sauté until thoroughly browned and the fat has dissolved under the skin, 15-20 minutes. Turn pieces over and brown other side.

Meanwhile cook fruits: simmer apples, apricots and prunes in stock until soft but not mushy, 10-15 minutes. Drain and reserve stock.

When duck is brown on both sides, discard excess fat from pan. Add stock from fruit, cover and simmer over low heat, stirring occasionally, until duck is tender, 15-20 minutes. If pan gets dry during cooking, add more stock.

To finish: remove pieces of duck and keep warm. Strain sauce into a saucepan, add lemon juice and taste for seasoning. Take from heat and add remaining butter in small pieces, shaking the pan to mix them into the sauce. Reheat fruit in the sauce.

Cut each duck breast into diagonal slices and discard bone. On individual plates arrange a piece of duck leg and a few slices of breast with a selection of fruits. Spoon sauce over duck, sprinkle with toasted almonds and serve at once.

### GETTING AHEAD
Duck and fruits can be cooked up to 48 hours ahead. Reheat duck in a 180°C/350°F/gas 4 oven. Finish the sauce just before serving, add fruit and assemble.

### VARIATION
*Sauté of Pork Chops with Dried Fruits* (Sauté de côtes de porc agenaise)
Substitute 4 pork chops for the duck. Brown them in oil and butter, cover pan and cook gently for 20-30 minutes, turning occasionally. Add stock and fruit and continue cooking as for duck.

---

# SAUTE OF PIGEON WITH CARAMELIZED ONION

## SAUTE DE PIGEONNEAUX AUX OIGNONS CONFITS

The onions are caramelized by sautéing them until they are soft and glazed and then cooking them with sugar to a rich brown.

### SERVES 4

| | |
|---|---|
| 4 pigeons | ¾ pt/450 ml water |
| 1 tablespoon oil | salt and pepper |
| 1 tablespoon butter | **For caramelized onions** |
| **For stock** | 2 lb/1 kg baby onions, peeled |
| 1 tablespoon oil | ¾ pt/450 ml water |
| giblets and trimmings from pigeons | 1½ oz/40 g butter |
| 1 onion, sliced | 2½ oz/65 g sugar |
| 1 carrot, sliced | bouquet garni* |

With poultry scissors or a sharp knife, cut the birds in half along the breastbone. Remove the backbone and trim off wingtips. Reserve giblets.

For stock: in a medium saucepan heat oil and sauté giblets, backbones and wingtips until they start to brown. Add onion and carrot; brown thoroughly. Add bouquet garni, water and a little salt and pepper; bring to the boil. Simmer until liquid is reduced to half, ¾-1 hour. Strain and reserve.

For caramelized onions: put onions, water, butter and all but 2 tablespoons sugar in a saucepan. Bring to the boil and simmer until water has evaporated and onions are tender, 20-25 minutes. Transfer onions to a sauté pan, sprinkle with remaining sugar and cook over brisk heat until the sugar caramelizes, shaking the pan so the onions colour evenly. They should be dark brown and soft but still hold their shape.

To sauté pigeons heat oil and butter in the sauté pan until foaming. Season pigeon halves and add them, skin side down, to the pan – it should be large enough for all birds to touch the bottom. Cover and sauté over medium heat until browned, 10-15 minutes. Turn birds over, add half the stock and continue cooking until done, about 5 minutes for pink meat or 10-15 minutes for well done.

Remove pigeon and keep warm. Add remaining stock to pan and boil, stirring to dissolve pan juices. Strain into a saucepan, skim off excess fat, taste for seasoning and reheat. Meanwhile reheat onions.

Arrange pigeon on a serving dish or on individual plates and put onions on one side. Spoon a little gravy over pigeon and serve the rest separately.

### GETTING AHEAD
Onions can be cooked up to 3 days ahead. Pigeons can be halved and stock made up to 8 hours ahead. Cook and serve pigeon at the last minute.

### VARIATION
*Sauté of Pigeon with Glazed Turnips* (Sauté de pigeonneaux aux navets glacés)
Substitute 2 lb/1 kg baby turnips for the onions. Peel them and trim into olive shapes. Cook in butter, water and sugar, as for onions, until tender and glazed, 15-20 minutes. Do not add extra sugar to caramelize turnips.

# Veal Escalopes Sauteed with Port

## ESCALOPES DE VEAU SAUTEES AU PORTO

Look for veal that is pale pink and shiny, showing it is young and freshly cut. Ask the butcher to flatten the escalopes and trim them to a neat shape.

### SERVES 4

| | |
|---|---|
| ½ lb/250 g fresh tagliatelle | 2 tablespoons oil |
| 4 veal escalopes, about 3 oz/75 g each | 1 oz/25 g butter |
| 2 tablespoons flour, more if necessary | 2½ fl oz/65 ml port |
| salt and pepper | 4 fl oz/125 ml veal stock* or water |
| | 8 fl oz/250 ml brown sauce (p. 12) |

Put noodles in a large pan of boiling salted water and cook until tender but still firm, 3-5 minutes. Drain, rinse with hot water to wash away starch and return to pan. Add hot water to cover and leave to keep warm.

Season flour with salt and pepper and coat escalopes with it, patting to discard the excess.

In a sauté pan heat oil and butter until foaming. Add escalopes and sauté over medium heat 1-2 minutes on each side until brown. Escalopes should not overlap; sauté in two batches if necessary. Discard excess fat, add half the port and flame*.

Add stock to pan and boil, stirring to dissolve juices. Stir in brown sauce and bring to the boil. Replace escalopes and simmer until tender, 5-7 minutes. Remove them and keep warm.

Strain sauce into a saucepan, add remaining port, reheat and taste for seasoning.

Overlap escalopes on a serving dish or put on individual plates and spoon a little of the sauce over

them. Drain noodles, add to remaining sauce and toss. Spoon noodles beside escalopes and serve.

### GETTING AHEAD
Both escalopes and noodles are best cooked just before serving.

### VARIATION
*Sauté of Ham with Port* (Sauté de jambon au porto) Substitute 4 thick slices cooked ham for the veal. Coat in flour and sauté as for escalopes.

# Saute of Pheasant in Red Wine

## FAISAN SAUTE AU POMEROL

Pomerol is one of the better Bordeaux wines, but any dry, full-bodied red wine will do.

### SERVES 4-6

| | |
|---|---|
| 2 pheasants, each about 2 lb/1 kg | bones from the pheasants |
| 1 tablespoon oil | 1 mushroom, sliced |
| 1 oz/25 g butter | 2 shallots, diced |
| salt and pepper | 1 carrot, diced |
| ¼ lb/125 g mushrooms | ½ stalk celery, diced |
| 4 fl oz/125 ml red wine | bouquet garni* |
| fried croûtes* | ¾ pt/450 ml red wine |
| 1 tablespoon brandy | ¾ pt/450 ml brown stock* |
| few sprigs of parsley (for decoration) | 2 teaspoons arrowroot* mixed with 2 tablespoons water |
| **For sauce** | |
| 1 tablespoon oil | |

Cut pheasant into 4 pieces*, reserving the carcasses, wings and necks. Coarsely chop the reserved pieces.

For the sauce: heat oil in a heavy saucepan, add bones and brown thoroughly over high heat, stirring occasionally. Add mushroom, shallots, carrot and celery and continue to sauté until vegetables begin to brown. Add bouquet garni and enough wine to cover. Simmer until mixture is almost dry. Add remaining wine, stock and a little salt and pepper. Simmer until sauce is reduced to half, $\frac{1}{2}$-$\frac{3}{4}$ hour.

Meanwhile cook the pheasant: in sauté pan heat oil and butter over medium heat until foaming. Season pheasant pieces, add to pan and brown, turning from time to time, about 10 minutes.

Trim mushroom stems level with caps and add trimmings to sauce. Add mushroom caps to pheasant with red wine. Cover and cook over low heat stirring occasionally, until pheasant is tender when pierced with a fork: 20-25 minutes.

Make croûtes, big enough to put a piece of pheasant on. When pheasant is done, remove lid, add brandy and flame*. Place pheasant and mushrooms on croûtes on individual plates and keep warm.

Strain sauce into sauté pan and bring to the boil, stirring to dissolve pan juices. Strain back into saucepan. To thicken sauce: bring it back to the boil. Whisk in arrowroot paste, adding just enough so sauce is syrupy in consistency. Taste again for seasoning.

Spoon a little of the sauce over the pheasant and serve the rest separately. Decorate each piece of pheasant with a sprig of parsley.

### GETTING AHEAD
Pheasant and sauce can be cooked a day ahead and kept, covered, in the refrigerator. Reheat them together in a sauté pan. Thicken the sauce just before serving.

### VARIATION
*Sauté of Pheasant with Bacon, Mushrooms and Red Wine* (Sauté de faisan bourguignonne)
Substitute a Burgundy wine for the Bordeaux. Fry 2 oz/50 g smoked bacon, cut in dice, in 1 tablespoon oil until lightly browned. Take out, add 18 baby onions, peeled, and sauté until brown. Drain and add with bacon to pheasant at same time as mushrooms.

# SAUTE OF TURNIPS WITH ONIONS

## SAUTE DE NAVETS LYONNAISE

A sauté of turnips can be served as a first course, or as an accompaniment to roast or grilled meats; it is particularly good with lamb and beef.

### SERVES 4

| | |
|---|---|
| 1½ lemons | 4 fl oz/125 ml veal or chicken stock* or water, more if necessary |
| 1½ lb/750 g small turnips | |
| 1 oz/25 g butter | |
| 2 large onions, thinly sliced | 1 teaspoon tomato purée |
| | bouquet garni* |
| 1 tablespoon flour | salt and pepper |
| 2 fl oz/50 ml white wine | |

Peel turnips, quarter them if large and round off edges. Cook in boiling, salted water for 5 minutes, then drain.

In a sauté pan or a shallow flameproof casserole melt butter. Add onions, cover and cook over very low heat until soft but not brown, 15-20 minutes. Stir in flour, add wine, stock, tomato purée, bouquet garni, salt and pepper and bring just to the boil.

Put the turnips in the pan, cover and simmer until very tender, 35-45 minutes. Stir occasionally during cooking and add more stock, but only a little at a time, if turnips are dry. At the end of cooking only a few tablespoons of liquid should remain.

Discard bouquet garni and taste sauce for seasoning. Serve turnips in casserole, or transfer them to a serving dish or individual plates.

### GETTING AHEAD
The sauté can be cooked up to 2 days ahead and refrigerated, or frozen for up to 3 months. Reheat on top of the stove.

# 5
# BRAISES AND RAGOUTS

A braise or ragoût, to me, epitomises the best in French cooking, for it adds up to so much more than the sum of its parts. Starting point is a substantial cut of meat that is too tough or lean to roast – beef rump or round, shoulder of pork, or perhaps a casserole hen. The best cuts contain plenty of gelatine, which dissolves during the long cooking and adds richness to the sauce. For a braise the meat is left whole; for a ragoût it is cut in large cubes of up to 2 in/5 cm so it does not shrink too much during cooking. This main ingredient is cooked in the steady heat of a low oven with liquid and generous quantities of vegetables, so flavours mellow and a delectable sauce results.

The first step in assembling a braise, and many ragoûts, is to prepare a mirepoix, an aromatic base of diced onion and carrot and sometimes celery. The size of the mirepoix depends on the cooking time, varying from pea size for half-hour vegetable braises to 2 in/5 cm chunks appropriate to large pieces of beef and game which can take 3 hours or more in the oven. The fun begins with the selection of suitable flavourings. A touch of garlic with a few shallots is *de rigueur* for poultry and meat, as well as a bouquet garni and peppercorns. Other possibilities include juniper berries (for game), cloves (with meats), tomato purée (with pork and some vegetables) and even apples (with pork and red cabbage).

To keep the meat moist during cooking, stock is ideal, though water will do instead; often wine is called for, and it is not unusual to add a spoonful of vinegar for sharpness. At the beginning of cooking, the ingredients of a ragoût should swim in liquid so they are completely covered, to a third or half its depth, so it cooks partly in steam. Liquid evaporates during cooking so that ideally when the meat is tender, the sauce is just the right thickness after reducing by a third or half. Of course, this cannot be precisely controlled and more liquid must sometimes be added during cooking if the meat looks dry. Alternatively, if the finished sauce is too thin, it must be boiled, once the meat has been removed, to reduce it before serving.

The big question is what consistency is ideal. I'm a partisan of traditional sauces thickened with flour (or occasionally with vegetable purée) that generously coat the back of a spoon and give body to the dish. The current trend towards lighter cuisine calls for thickening with arrowroot or potato starch, or even for leaving the sauce very thin if plenty of cream is added.

A heavy-based casserole is important for long slow cooking and for most recipes it must be flameproof as the meat and vegetables are first browned on top of the stove. It can be made of tinned copper, stainless steel, enamelled cast iron, aluminium or plain cast iron, in descending order of cost. Provided the pan has a really heavy base, the material is less important than how it is used: heat should be medium on top of the stove and low and steady in the oven. Make sure the lid fits tightly and choose a size, large or small, oval or round, to fit the ingredients.

36

Unpleasantly harsh before it is cooked, the flavour of a braise or ragoût mellows – the transformation of a typical beef and vegetable recipe during its two to three hours in the oven is hard to believe. Seasoning is deceptive and it is important to taste the sauce just before serving. When done, a skewer inserted in a large piece of meat should be hot to the touch when withdrawn, while smaller pieces should fall easily from a two-pronged fork without clinging. Chefs, who seem to have heatproof hands, like to pinch the meat to see if it crushes easily; vegetables should be quite soft and only fish should remain firm-textured. Braises and ragoûts, especially with meat, mellow if kept a day or two in the refrigerator, and they freeze well.

Given the importance of the sauce, accompaniments should display a braise or ragoût to advantage. Rice marries with almost any recipe and homemade noodles have recently become the fashion, particularly with fish. Boiled or mashed potatoes are an obvious choice, and in the French countryside you will be served sautéed potatoes with dishes like braised beef in red wine and ragoût of duck.

# BRAISED CHICKEN WITH ONIONS AND MUSHROOMS

## POULET BRAISE A L'ANCIENNE

Any dish 'à l'ancienne' is rich, usually in a sauce thickened with egg yolks and cream. This recipe is designed for a mature hen, but a roasting chicken can be used instead.

### SERVES 4

| | |
|---|---|
| 1 large hen or a roasting chicken, about 4 lb/2 kg, trussed* | 1 tablespoon parsley |
| | **For garnish** |
| 1 tablespoon oil | ½ lb/250 g baby onions, peeled |
| 1 tablespoon butter | ½ lb/250 g baby mushrooms, quartered |
| 1 onion, chopped | |
| 1 carrot, chopped | juice of ½ lemon |
| 1 tablespoon flour | 2 fl oz/50 ml water |
| 1 shallot, chopped | **For sauce** |
| ¾ pt/450 ml chicken stock*, more if needed | 1½ oz/40 g butter |
| 8 fl oz/250 ml white wine | 3 tablespoons flour |
| bouquet garni* | 4 fl oz/125 ml crème fraîche* or double cream |
| salt and pepper | 2 egg yolks |

Set oven at 180°C/350°F/gas 4. In a casserole heat oil and butter. Cook bird lightly on all sides so it whitens but does not brown. Take out, add onion and carrot and sauté until soft. Stir in flour and cook, stirring, until foaming but not brown. Replace chicken on its side, add shallot, stock, wine, bouquet garni, salt and pepper. Cover and bring to the boil.

Braise in oven 1-1¼ hours for a chicken or 1½-1¾ hours for a hen. During cooking, turn bird from one thigh to the other and finally onto its back. To test, pierce thigh with a skewer; juices should run clear, not pink.

Meanwhile prepare garnish: cook baby onions in boiling salted water, covered, until tender, 12-15 minutes. Drain them. Put mushrooms in a pan with lemon juice, water, salt and pepper. Cover and boil until tender, 4-6 minutes.

Transfer chicken to a serving dish and keep warm. Skim excess fat from cooking liquid.

For sauce: melt butter in a saucepan. Stir in flour and cook until foaming. Let cool slightly and strain in cooking liquid. Bring to the boil, whisking until sauce thickens. Simmer 2 minutes. Add onions and mushrooms with their liquid and heat gently.

In a small bowl, stir cream with egg yolks and add a little of the hot sauce to the cream mixture. Stir cream mixture back into the saucepan, off the heat. Heat gently until sauce thickens slightly, but do not boil or it will curdle. Take from heat and taste for seasoning.

Carve chicken into 8 pieces* or leave it whole. Arrange on a serving dish or individual plates and spoon mushrooms and onions over chicken. Sprinkle with chopped parsley and serve remaining sauce separately.

### GETTING AHEAD

Chicken with sauce and garnish can be prepared a day ahead and kept covered in the refrigerator, or frozen. Undercook chicken slightly to allow for reheating in the oven. Add egg yolks and cream just before serving.

### VARIATION

*Braised Chicken with Onions, Mushrooms and Bacon* (Poulet braisé bonne femme)
Add to onion and mushroom garnish, 6 oz/175 g diced bacon and sauté until lightly browned. Omit egg yolks and cream from sauce.

# BRAISED BEEF WITH RED WINE

## BŒUF BRAISE BOURGUIGNON

In this version of the famous Burgundian red wine stew, the meat is left in one piece. Topside and rump are good cuts to use.

### SERVES 8

| | |
|---|---|
| 4 lb/2 kg piece of beef | 1 clove garlic, crushed |
| 2 tablespoons oil | 6 peppercorns |
| 3 tablespoons flour | 2 cloves |
| 8 fl oz/250 ml beef stock*, more if needed | pinch of salt |
| salt and pepper | 2 tablespoons oil |
| 1 tablespoon chopped parsley (for sprinkling) | **For garnish** |
| **For marinade** | 2 tablespoons oil |
| 1 bottle/75 cl red Burgundy wine | ½ lb/250 g piece of bacon, diced |
| 1 onion, sliced | ½ lb/250 g baby onions, peeled |
| 1 carrot, sliced | ½ lb/250 g mushrooms, quartered |
| bouquet garni* | |

To marinate* meat: 2-3 days before cooking, combine ingredients for marinade in a saucepan, bring to the boil, simmer 10 minutes and leave to cool. Put meat in a deep bowl and pour cold marinade over meat so it is almost covered. Cover and keep in refrigerator 2-3 days, turning meat from time to time.

Drain meat, reserving marinade: keep onion and carrot separate. Dry meat thoroughly with paper towels. Set oven at 160°C/325°F/gas 3.

In a casserole heat 2 tablespoons oil and brown meat very thoroughly on all sides. Take out, add reserved onion and carrot and cook until soft but not brown. Lower heat. Add flour and cook, stirring, until it and vegetables are very brown. Stir in the remaining marinade ingredients and replace the meat. Add stock, salt and pepper. Cover and bring to the boil.

Braise beef in heated oven until tender when pierced with a two-pronged fork, 3-4 hours. If pan gets dry during cooking, add more stock.

For garnish: in a frying pan heat oil and fry bacon until lightly browned but not crisp. Remove, add onions and brown them also. Take them out and sauté mushrooms until brown.

When beef is tender, lift it out and strain sauce. If thin, boil sauce until reduced and rich; if thick, add more stock. Wipe out casserole and replace beef and sauce. Add garnish, heat gently and taste for seasoning. Cover and continue cooking 10-15 minutes so flavours blend.

Transfer beef to a carving board and discard strings. Carve in thick slices. Arrange slices, overlapping, on a serving dish or individual plates. Spoon garnish and a little sauce over meat. Sprinkle with parsley. Serve remaining sauce separately.

### GETTING AHEAD
Beef and garnish can be prepared up to 2 days ahead and refrigerated in separate containers. They can also be frozen. Reheat beef in oven or on top of stove, and then add garnish and cook gently to allow flavours to blend.

### VARIATION
*Braised Beef with Mushrooms* (Bœuf braisé chasseur) Substitute 1 pt/600 ml white wine for the red. Omit bacon and add double quantity of mushrooms to sauce with 1 tablespoon tomato purée.

# BRAISED SHOULDER OF LAMB WITH HAM AND PEPPERS

### EPAULE D'AGNEAU BRAISEE BASQUAISE
A dish to serve hot or cold.

#### SERVES 8

| | |
|---|---|
| *4-5 lb/2-2.5 g shoulder of lamb, boned so that a pocket is formed, with the bones* | *1 carrot, diced* |
| | *3/4 pt/450 ml veal stock\*, more if needed* |
| *salt and pepper* | **For garnish** |
| *2 cloves garlic, crushed* | *3 green peppers* |
| *1 teaspoon thyme* | *3 red peppers* |
| *1 teaspoon rosemary* | *3 tablespoons oil* |
| *4 thin slices cooked ham* | *1 clove garlic, crushed* |
| *1 tablespoon oil* | *1 tablespoon wine vinegar (if serving cold)* |
| *1 onion, diced* | |

Cut meat to open pocket so it lies flat. Trim off any skin and all but a thin layer of fat. Lay meat, skin side down, on work surface. Sprinkle meat with salt and pepper, garlic, thyme and rosemary. Lay ham slices on top of seasonings, roll meat into a neat cylinder and tie with string. Preheat oven to 180°C/350°F/gas 4.

Heat oil in a casserole and brown meat on all sides, with the bones. Take out meat. Add onion and carrot and brown them. Replace meat on top of bones and vegetables. Pour over stock, season and bring to the boil. Cover and braise in oven 1-1¼ hours for pink lamb or 1½-1¾ hours for well done meat. Test with a skewer\*. If the casserole gets dry during cooking, add more stock.

For garnish: grill peppers, turning from time to time, until their skins are blistered on all sides. Remove and cover with a damp cloth. Let cool.

Peel, core and seed peppers and cut into thick strips. Heat oil in a sauté pan and add peppers, garlic, salt and pepper. Sauté, stirring, until the peppers are tender but not brown, 3-4 minutes.

If serving meat hot: transfer to a board and leave 10-15 minutes so juices are reabsorbed. For gravy, strain the cooking liquid into a small saucepan, boil until reduced to a syrupy consistency, skim off fat with a spoon and taste for seasoning. Discard trussing strings. Carve lamb into ⅜ in/1 cm slices and arrange them, overlapping, on a serving dish or individual plates. Spoon pepper garnish around meat and serve gravy separately.

If serving cold: let lamb cool completely before slicing. Toss sautéed peppers with vinegar before spooning them around meat. Keep cooking juices to add to stock pot.

### GETTING AHEAD

Lamb and peppers can be prepared and refrigerated up to 2 days ahead. If serving hot, undercook slightly to allow for reheating. Reheat lamb in oven and peppers on top of stove.

### VARIATIONS

*Braised Loin of Pork with Ham and Peppers* (Carré de porc braisée basquaise)
Substitute 3 lb/1.5 kg boned loin of pork for lamb. Slit pork horizontally, so that it will lie flat. Roll and add ham as for lamb and braise 1½-2 hours until well done when tested with a skewer*.
*Braised Breast of Veal with Ham and Peppers* (Poitrine de veau braisée basquaise)
Substitute a boned breast. Braise 1½-1¾ hours until well done when tested with a skewer*.

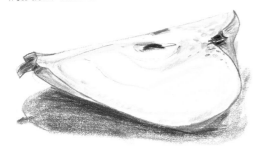

# LEG OF LAMB AS VENISON

## GIGOT D'AGNEAU EN CHEVREUIL

When a leg of lamb is marinated* for 2 or 3 days, with a bit of imagination it tastes like venison. Serve it with game accompaniments like braised red cabbage with chestnuts (p. 43) or celeriac purée (p. 56).

### SERVES 6-8

| | |
|---|---|
| 5-6 lb/2.5-3 kg leg of lamb | 2 carrots, sliced |
| ½ lb/250 g piece fat bacon, cut in strips (for larding*) | 4 shallots, sliced |
| | bouquet garni* |
| | 2 cloves garlic, peeled |
| 2 tablespoons oil | 2 tablespoons oil |
| 2 oz/50 g butter | pinch of salt |
| 8 fl oz/250 ml stock*, more if needed | pinch of sugar |
| salt and pepper | 2 teaspoons black peppercorns |
| 1 teaspoon arrowroot* mixed to a paste with 1 tablespoon cold water | 10 juniper berries, crushed |
| **For marinade** | **For garnish** |
| 1 bottle/75 cl red Bordeaux wine | 2 lb/1 kg firm pears |
| | 1 oz/25 g butter |
| 2½ fl oz/65 ml red wine vinegar | 2 tablespoons sugar |
| | 4 oz/125 g redcurrant jelly |
| 2 onions, sliced | |

To marinate* meat: 2-3 days before cooking, combine all ingredients for marinade in a saucepan, bring to the boil, simmer 10 minutes and leave to cool. Lard* meat with bacon and set in a deep bowl. Pour cold marinade over meat so it is covered. Cover bowl and keep in refrigerator 2-3 days, turning meat from time to time.

Drain meat, reserving marinade, and keep vegetables separate. Dry meat thoroughly with paper towels. Preheat oven to 180°C/350°F/gas 4.

In a casserole heat oil and half the butter and brown lamb as evenly as possible. Take it out, add reserved vegetables and brown them also. Replace lamb and stir in remaining marinade ingredients, stock, salt and pepper. Cover and bring to the boil.

Braise in oven, allowing 1¼-1½ hours for pink lamb, or 1½-2 hours for well done meat. Test with a skewer*. If the pan gets dry during cooking, add more stock.

For garnish: peel, halve and core pears. Set in a baking dish, dot with butter and sprinkle with sugar. Add 3 or 4 spoonfuls of cooking liquid from lamb. Bake pears in oven with lamb, basting often, until tender, 20-30 minutes.

Transfer lamb to a board and leave 10-15 minutes so juices are reabsorbed. Strain cooking liquid and skim off excess fat. Boil until reduced to about 8 fl oz/250 ml. Whisk arrowroot paste into boiling liquid so it thickens slightly. Take sauce from heat, whisk in remaining butter in small pieces and taste for seasoning. Keep warm.

Carve lamb and reshape pieces on the bone, or carve meat at the table. Set the leg on a serving dish. Fill hollow in each pear with a spoonful of redcurrant jelly and arrange pears around lamb. Serve the sauce separately.

### GETTING AHEAD
Lamb and pears can be cooked up to 2 days ahead; undercook them slightly to allow for reheating. Both should be kept in the refrigerator and reheated in the oven. Add butter to sauce just before serving.

### VARIATION
*Loin of Pork as Wild Boar* (Carré de porc en sanglier) Substitute 4½ lb/2-2¼ kg pork loin, on the bone, for leg of lamb. Braise 2-2½ hours or until pork is well done when tested with a skewer*.

# BRAISED SWEET-SOUR PORK WITH APRICOTS

## PORC BRAISE A L'AIGRE-DOUX AUX ABRICOTS

A mixture of caramel and vinegar is often used to give a sweet-sour touch to dishes like duck with oranges and this braised pork with apricots.

### SERVES 6-8

| | |
|---|---|
| 2 tablespoons oil | salt and pepper |
| 3 lb/1.5 kg boned loin or shoulder of pork, with the bones | ½ lb/250 g dried apricots, soaked overnight and drained |
| 1 onion, diced | 2 teaspoons arrowroot dissolved in 2 tablespoons cold water |
| 1 carrot, diced | |
| ¾ pt/450 ml veal stock*, more if needed | 1 oz/25 g butter |
| 1 shallot, diced | **For caramel** |
| 1 clove garlic, crushed | 1½ oz/40 g sugar |
| 2 teaspoons tomato paste | 2 fl oz/50 ml water |
| bouquet garni* | 2½ fl oz/65 ml white wine vinegar |

Preheat oven to 180°C/350°F/gas 4. In a casserole heat oil and brown pork on all sides with the bones. Take out meat, add onion and carrot and brown also. Replace meat and add stock, shallot, garlic, tomato purée, bouquet garni, salt and pepper. Cover and bring to the boil.

Braise in oven until tender when pierced with a two-pronged fork, 1½-2 hours. If the pan gets dry during cooking, add more stock.

For caramel: heat sugar with water until dissolved, then boil steadily to a light brown caramel. Take from heat. Cover your hand with a cloth to protect it and then pour in vinegar all at once. Stand back because vapour from the vinegar will make your eyes sting. Heat mixture gently until caramel is dissolved, take from heat and let it cool.

Remove pork from pan and keep warm. Strain cooking liquid into a saucepan and skim off excess fat. Add soaked apricots and simmer until tender, about 10 minutes. Drain apricots and reserve. If necessary, boil liquid until reduced to about 8 fl oz/ 250 ml.

Add caramel mixture to cooking liquid. Whisk arrowroot paste into boiling liquid until lightly thickened. Replace apricots and taste for seasoning. Take sauce from the heat and stir in butter, in small pieces. Keep warm.

Carve pork in ½ in/1 cm slices and arrange the slices, overlapping, on a serving dish or on individual plates. Spoon apricots and a little of the sauce around the meat and serve remaining sauce separately.

### GETTING AHEAD

Pork, apricots and sauce can be cooked up to 2 days ahead and kept in the refrigerator; they can also be frozen. Reheat them together in a casserole in the oven. Add butter to sauce just before serving.

### VARIATION

*Braised Sweet-Sour Duck with Apricots* (Canard braisé à l'aigre-doux aux abricots)
Substitute two 4 lb/2 kg ducks for the pork. Truss* ducks and brown them very thoroughly. Discard any fat before adding vegetables. Braise ducks until tender when pierced in the thigh with a two-pronged fork, 1¼-1½ hours.

# BRAISED RED CABBAGE WITH CHESTNUTS

## CHOU ROUGE BRAISE AUX MARRONS

The acid in vinegar and red wine helps keep cabbage a brilliant red.

### SERVES 6

| | |
|---|---|
| 1 lb/500 g chestnuts, peeled* | ¼ lb/125 g piece bacon, diced |
| 3 lb/1.5 kg head of red cabbage, coarsely shredded | 1 tart apple, peeled, cored and diced |
| | 1 bay leaf |
| 1 tablespoon wine vinegar | 1 onion, stuck with a clove |
| 2 teaspoons sugar | |
| salt and pepper | 6 fl oz/175 ml red wine |
| 3 tablespoons oil | |

Prepare chestnuts*. In a large bowl put cabbage, vinegar, sugar and a little salt and pepper. Mix well, cover and leave to marinate ½-1 hour.

Preheat oven to 160°C/325°F/gas 3. In a large casserole, heat half the oil. Add a third of the cabbage and cover with half the chestnuts, half the bacon and the apple. Add a second layer of cabbage, then more chestnuts and bacon. Cover with remaining cabbage. Pin bay leaf to onion with clove and bury it in cabbage. Top with remaining oil and wine. Cover and bring to the boil on top of stove.

Braise in oven until cabbage and chestnuts are tender, 1-1½ hours. The cabbage should remain firm. If cabbage is very moist, remove lid during last 15 minutes of cooking so that moisture evaporates.

Discard onion and taste for seasoning; the cabbage should be quite peppery.

### GETTING AHEAD

Cabbage can be cooked up to 3 days ahead and

refrigerated; the flavour improves if it is kept at least 24 hours. Undercook it slightly to allow for reheating in oven or on top of stove.

### VARIATION

*Braised Red Cabbage with Onions* (Chou rouge braisé aux oignons)
Substitute 1 lb/500 g baby onions for chestnuts and omit whole onion and clove.

---

# BRAISED LETTUCE

## LAITUES BRAISEES

A splendid recipe for summer.

---

### SERVES 4

| | |
|---|---|
| 2-4 heads cos lettuce, depending on size | 8 fl oz/250 ml veal or chicken stock* |
| 1 oz/30 g butter | salt and pepper |
| 2 rashers bacon | 1 tablespoon chopped parsley |
| 6 oz/180 g baby onions, peeled | |

---

Preheat oven to 180°C/350°F/gas 4. Wash lettuces, keeping them whole and trimming each base without detaching the outer leaves. If they are very large, cut them in half lengthwise.

Blanch* lettuces in boiling salted water for 5 minutes. Drain them. Rinse with cold water and drain thoroughly.

Thickly butter a casserole, lay the bacon in the bottom and sprinkle with baby onions. Fold tops of lettuces under to make neat bundles and lay them on the bacon and onions. Pour stock over lettuces and sprinkle with salt and pepper. Cover with buttered paper and then with lid.

Braise in heated oven until tender, about 45-55 minutes.

Drain the lettuces, pressing with a spatula to extract cooking liquid. Reserve liquid. Arrange lettuces and onions on a serving dish and keep warm.

Strain cooking liquid into a small pan and boil until reduced to a syrupy glaze. If you like, chop up bacon and sprinkle it over the lettuces.

Taste liquid for seasoning. Pour it over lettuces, sprinkle with parsley and serve.

### GETTING AHEAD

Lettuces can be cooked up to 2 days in advance and refrigerated. Undercook them slightly to allow for reheating in the oven.

### VARIATIONS

*Braised Celery* (Céleri braisé)
Substitute 1 stick of celery for the lettuce. Cut into 3 in/7 cm lengths and discard the leaves. If celery stalks are tough, peel strings from the outside with a vegetable peeler.

*Braised Chicory* (Endive braisée)
Substitute 1½ lb/750 g chicory for the lettuce. Do not blanch chicory. There will be little cooking liquid so reducing is not necessary.

---

# RAGOUT OF DUCK WITH ORANGES

## RAGOUT DE CANARD A L'ORANGE

Be sure to brown the duck thoroughly so fat runs from under the skin before adding onions.

---

### SERVES 6-8

| | |
|---|---|
| 2 ducks, 4 lb/2 kg each | 1¼ pt/750 ml veal stock*, more if needed |
| salt and pepper | bouquet garni* |
| 2 tablespoons oil | 5 small seedless oranges |
| 2 onions, chopped | 2 tablespoons Grand Marnier |
| 2 tablespoons flour | |

---

Cut each duck into 4 pieces*. Sprinkle the 8 pieces with salt and pepper.

In a large sauté pan or shallow flameproof

casserole heat oil over medium heat. Add duck pieces, skin side down. Sauté until well browned, 15-20 minutes. Fat should be rendered so that duck is not greasy. Turn and brown other side.

Remove duck and discard all but 1 tablespoon of fat from the pan. Lower heat and add onions. Sauté, stirring occasionally, until soft but not brown. Stir in flour and cook until browned. Pour in stock, add bouquet garni, season and bring just to the boil. Return duck to pan, cover and simmer until duck is tender when pierced with a fork, 20-30 minutes. If sauce gets thick during cooking, add more stock.

Meanwhile, cut skin and pith from 2 of the oranges with a sharp knife. Cut between segments and scoop them out, discarding the membrane. Put segments in a small pan with Grand Marnier. Pare rind from remaining oranges with a vegetable peeler, leaving behind all the white pith, and cut the rind into fine julienne* strips. Blanch* rind by putting in cold water and boiling 2 minutes to remove bitterness; drain. Squeeze juice from orange flesh and reserve it.

When duck pieces are cooked, remove them from pan and trim knuckle bones. Skim any fat from sauce. Sauce should be thick enough to generously coat a spoon; if too thin, boil until reduced and thickened. Stir in orange juice and strips of rind. Replace the pieces of duck and bring just back to the boil.

Meanwhile gently heat orange segments. Drain the Grand Marnier from them and stir into the sauce; it should lightly coat a spoon. Taste the sauce for seasoning.

Arrange pieces of duck on a serving plate or individual plates. Spoon a little sauce over them and decorate with orange segments. Serve remaining sauce separately.

## GETTING AHEAD

Duck can be cooked 48 hours ahead and refrigerated in the sauce, or it can be frozen. Orange strips, juice and segments can be prepared in the morning for the evening. Reheat duck on top of stove, add orange juice and complete sauce just before serving.

# RAGOUT OF ONIONS WITH RED WINE

## RAGOUT D'OIGNONS AU VIN ROUGE

Serve with either hot or cold roast duck or pork.

### SERVES 4

| | |
|---|---|
| 1 tablespoon oil | 1 oz/25 g raisins |
| 8 medium onions, peeled | 2 tomatoes, peeled, seeded and chopped* |
| 2 tablespoons flour | |
| 4 fl oz/125 ml red wine | bouquet garni* |
| 12 fl oz/350 ml veal or chicken stock*, more if needed | salt and pepper |

Set oven at 180°C/350°F/gas 4. In a shallow casserole heat oil and brown onions, shaking the pan so they colour evenly. Sprinkle with flour and allow it to brown. Add wine, stock, raisins, tomatoes, bouquet garni, salt and pepper and bring to the boil.

Cover and cook in oven, basting from time to time, until onions are tender, 1¼-1½ hours. Remove lid towards end of cooking so sauce reduces until lightly thickened and onions brown on top.

Taste sauce for seasoning. Serve onions hot or at room temperature.

### GETTING AHEAD

Onions can be cooked up to 3 days ahead and refrigerated. Gently reheat them on top of the stove.

### VARIATION

*Ragoût of Mushrooms with Red Wine* (Ragoût de champignons au vin rouge)
Substitute 1½ lb/750 g mushrooms for onions. Use only 8 fl oz/250 ml of stock and omit raisins. Cook mushrooms until tender, 10-15 minutes.

Turnips or Jerusalem artichokes can also be substituted for the onions and raisins. Turnips cook in 30-40 minutes; artichokes in 20-30 minutes.

# DAUBE OF LAMB WITH TOMATO AND OLIVES

## DAUBE D'AGNEAU PROVENÇALE

A daube is another name for ragoût, deriving from the earthenware 'daubière' pots that were used in Provence.

### SERVES 8

| | |
|---|---|
| 4 lb/2 kg boned shoulder of lamb | 2 lb/1 kg tomatoes, peeled, seeded and chopped* |
| 3 tablespoons oil | |
| 4 onions, sliced | 4 cloves garlic, crushed |
| 3 tablespoons flour | bouquet garni* |
| 12 fl oz/350 ml white wine | pared rind of 2 oranges cut in long strips |
| 12 fl oz/350 ml veal or beef stock*, more if needed | salt and pepper |
| | 4 oz/125 g green olives |
| | 4 oz/125 g black olives |

Set oven at 160°C/325°F/gas 3. Trim lamb of all fat and sinew and cut into 1½ in/4 cm cubes.

In a flameproof casserole heat the oil and brown the lamb pieces, a few at a time, on all sides. Remove meat. Add onions to casserole and sauté, stirring occasionally, until they begin to brown. Stir in flour and brown also. Add wine, stock, tomatoes, garlic, bouquet garni, orange rind, salt and pepper. Return lamb to casserole, stir to mix and bring just to the boil.

Cover and cook in the oven until meat is very tender when pierced with a fork, 1½-2 hours. Stir from time to time during cooking and add more stock if lamb looks dry.

Blanch* olives to remove excess salt: put them in a pan of cold water, bring to the boil and simmer 3-4 minutes. Drain.

Ten minutes before end of cooking, discard bouquet garni and orange rind from lamb and stir in olives. Taste for seasoning. If sauce is thin, remove lid during this final cooking. Serve daube in the casserole.

### GETTING AHEAD

Daube can be cooked 3 days ahead and refrigerated, or frozen. Reheat it on top of the stove.

### VARIATIONS

*Daube of Beef with Tomato and Olives* (Daube de bœuf provençale)
Substitute 4 lb/2 kg beef rump. Cut beef in 2 in/5 cm cubes and cook until very tender, 2½-3 hours.
*Daube of Guinea Fowl with Tomato and Olives* (Daube de pintade provençale)
Substitute 3 guinea fowl, each weighing about 3 lb/1.5 kg, for the lamb. Cut each bird into 4 pieces*. Use only 8 fl oz/250 ml of wine and simmer birds until tender, 30-40 minutes.

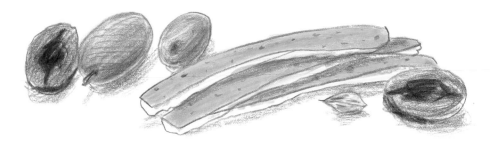

# BLANQUETTE OF VEAL

## BLANQUETTE DE VEAU

Traditionally blanquette is made with the whole breast of veal, which contains bones for flavour and gelatine for richness, plus some veal shoulder to add solid meat. Serve it with boiled rice.

### SERVES 6

| | |
|---|---|
| 1 lb/500 g boneless veal shoulder, cut in 2 in/5 cm pieces | salt and white pepper |
| 2 lb/1 kg veal breast, including bones, cut in chunks | **For garnish** |
| | 1 oz/25 g butter |
| | ½ lb/250 g baby onions, peeled |
| 2 onions, quartered and stuck with 1 clove | ½ lb/250 g mushrooms, quartered if large |
| 2 carrots, quartered | **For sauce** |
| bouquet garni* | 2 oz/50 g butter |
| 2⅓ pt/1.5 litres veal stock* or water, more if needed | 1 oz/25 g flour |
| | juice of ½ lemon |
| | grated nutmeg |

Trim sinew and any fat from meat.

To blanch veal: put it in a large pan, cover it with cold water and bring just to the boil. Simmer 5 minutes, drain and rinse.

Replace veal in the pan with bones, large onions, carrots, bouquet garni, enough stock or water to just cover, and a little salt and pepper. Cover pan and simmer until veal is very tender, 1¼-1½ hours, skimming occasionally.

For garnish: melt butter in a sauté pan, add onions with salt and pepper. Cover and cook over very low heat, shaking pan occasionally, until tender, 15-20 minutes. As a blanquette must be white, do not allow them to brown. Put mushrooms in a pan with salt, pepper and ½ in/1 cm of water.

Cover, bring to the boil and simmer for 5 minutes. Add cooking liquid to veal and put mushrooms with onions.

When veal is cooked, transfer it to a bowl, cover and keep warm. Boil stock until reduced to about 1¼ pt/750 ml.

For sauce: in a saucepan melt butter, stir in flour and cook until foaming but not browned. Strain in stock and bring to the boil, whisking constantly. Simmer until sauce is well flavoured and lightly coats the back of a spoon, 10-15 minutes.

Add veal, onions and mushrooms to the sauce and season to taste with lemon juice, nutmeg, salt and pepper. Heat gently without boiling for 5-10 minutes so flavours blend. Serve in a bowl.

### GETTING AHEAD

Veal, garnish and sauce can be prepared up to 48 hours ahead. Reheat it just before serving.

### VARIATIONS

*Blanquette of Veal with Cream* (Blanquette de veau à l'ancienne)

Shortly before serving veal, mix 2 egg yolks with 4 fl oz/125 ml crème fraîche* or double cream in a small bowl. Add a little hot sauce from veal, then stir mixture back into remaining blanquette, off the heat. Heat gently until sauce thickens slightly but do not boil or it will curdle. Serve at once.

*Blanquette of Veal with Mustard* (Blanquette de veau dijonnaise)

Before serving, stir 1-2 tablespoons Dijon mustard with 4 fl oz/125 ml crème fraîche* or double cream into sauce. Bring just back to the boil and taste.

# 6
# POT-AU-FEU

French pot-au-feu and potée, British boiled beef and hot pot, American boiled dinner all belong to the same family of meats that are cooked together in one large pot with generous quantities of vegetables. The broth from cooking makes a first course, while the meats and vegetables form a main dish. Despite, or perhaps because of, its country origins, pot-au-feu is the pride of many a Parisian bistro, whether it is the classic recipe based on beef, or the Provençal mutton version flavoured with garlic, or the poule au pot with a stuffed chicken from Béarn. Closely related is potée, made mainly with pork and cabbage, and the fish stews dubbed pot-au-feu by nouvelle cuisine chefs. These combine fish and vegetables in a rich broth and require shorter cooking time than the traditional recipes with meat.

You need a clear head, if not a pocket calculator, to cook the four meats and half-dozen vegetables of the classic pot-au-feu to perfection. Its quality depends on adding the main ingredients one by one to the broth at the right time, so that the flavours blend and develop but nothing overcooks. To use the term 'boiled' is inaccurate for the pot must be simmered gently so meats, and particularly vegetables, cook thoroughly without breaking up. Meats like veal and chicken are often blanched first to keep them white, and during the cooking the pot-au-feu should be skimmed constantly so the broth remains clear.

In the country, pot-au-feu is invariably made with water, but there is no denying that adding a classic stock is

an improvement. The type should match the meat – beef, veal, chicken or fish – and it need not be strong. Beware of adding too much salt, for it will be further concentrated when the broth is boiled at the end of cooking. Veal bones are often included in the pot for richness and the cartilage in cuts of meat like veal breast and beef shin are an advantage, for they dissolve during cooking to add gelatine to the broth.

So they cook evenly and don't fall apart, meats for simmering must be tied compactly with string (poultry is trussed). Vegetables are often tied in bundles too, and some cooks like to wrap them in muslin. A muslin bag makes peppercorns and herbs easy to remove, and it will prevent the marrow falling out of marrow bones. When done, meats should yield easily to the tines of a two-pronged fork, while vegetables should be firm but tender – nouvelle cuisine crispness is not appropriate here. Fish should just flake easily.

The traditional pot-au-feu and potées are a family feast and half their charm lies in an abundant variety of meats and vegetables; it is not worth making them for a few people. Accompaniments are as classic as the dishes themselves: croûtes of toasted bread or homemade noodles are served with the unthickened broth; mustard, horseradish, coarse salt and pickles add punch to the meat course.

Pot-au-feu is usually made in a stockpot or else in a large braising casserole.

48

# POT-AU-FEU OF FISH

## POT-AU-FEU HOUATAIS

Any variety of fish can be used for this fish stew, which is named after an island off the coast of Brittany. Monkfish, John Dory, bream, conger eel, hake and whiting are suggested.

### SERVES 8-10

| | |
|---|---|
| 3¼ pt/2 litres fish stock* | **For the vegetables** |
| 5 lb/2.5 kg mixed fish fillets, with heads and bones | 5 carrots |
| | 2 turnips |
| large pinch of saffron threads | 3-4 stalks celery |
| | 2 leeks |
| toasted croûtes* made with 1 loaf French bread | 1 small green cabbage |
| | ½ lb/250 g green beans |
| 2 lb/1 kg large prawns | ½ lb/250 g shelled or frozen green peas (optional) |
| salt and pepper | 3¼ pt/2 litres water |

Make fish stock using heads and bones of fish. Strain it and add saffron, crushed to powder.

To prepare vegetables: peel carrots, cut them in 3 in/7.5 cm lengths and tie in bundles. Peel and quarter turnips. Peel outer stalks of celery to remove strings; wash and tie in a bundle. Trim and split leeks, wash them thoroughly and tie in a bundle. Separate the cabbage leaves, discarding outer ones, wash and tie into a neat ball. String the beans.

To cook vegetables: bring a large pan of salted water to the boil. Add carrots and turnips, cover and simmer until tender, about 15 minutes. Remove them with a slotted spoon. Add celery and simmer until tender, 8-10 minutes. Remove and bring water back to the boil. Add peas and boil until tender, about 5 minutes. Lift out with a slotted spoon, add green beans and boil until tender, about 5 minutes. Remove beans and add leeks and cabbage to boiling liquid. Boil until tender, about 15 minutes. Take out vegetables.

Untie carrots, celery, leeks, and cabbage; cut celery and leeks into 1½ in/4 cm lengths and the cabbage into wedges. Arrange vegetables in mounds around the edge of a large heatproof serving dish, cover tightly with foil and keep warm. Make croûtes.

Pour fish stock into a large saucepan and fit a screen or drum sieve on top. Bring stock to the boil. Put firm fish fillets (such as monkfish and conger eel) in the steamer above the stock. Sprinkle with salt and pepper. Cover and steam until fish just flakes easily, ·8-10 minutes. Transfer fish to centre of serving dish, cover and keep warm. Steam delicate fish and prawns in the same way for 4-5 minutes. Transfer them to the serving dish also.

Taste fish stock for seasoning and serve it in bowls as a first course with toasted croûtes. Serve fish and vegetables as the main course.

### GETTING AHEAD

You can cook the vegetables and make the stock and croûtes up to 6 hours ahead. The fish must be steamed just before serving.

### VARIATIONS

*Fish Stew with Saffron* (Soupe de poisson au safran)
**Serves 6-8**
In pot-au-feu of fish, omit the vegetables. Serve fish in the stock as a stew, passing croûtes separately.

*Fish Stew with Cream* (Soupe de poisson à la crème)
**Serves 6-8**
In pot-au-feu of fish, omit the vegetables and saffron. Add 8 fl oz/250 ml crème fraîche* or double cream to the fish stock. Serve fish in the stock, adding 3-4 tablespoons chopped parsley just before serving. Pass croûtes separately.

# COUNTRY POT-AU-FEU

## POT-AU-FEU PAYSANNE

A good pot-au-feu should contain beef and veal on the bone, such as shin and blade bone, a meaty piece like brisket, and marrow bones, as well as a good variety of vegetables. It is traditionally served with piquant accompaniments – coarse salt, gherkins, horseradish sauce and choice of mustards.

### SERVES 8

| | |
|---|---|
| 3 lb/1.5 kg veal, on the bone | 4 qt/5 litres water |
| 2 lb/1 kg beef, on the bone | salt |
| 2 lb/1 kg meaty piece of beef | 1/4 lb/125 g very fine noodles **or** toasted croûtes* made with a small loaf of French bread |
| 2 onions, each studded with a clove | |
| 2 carrots | **For the vegetables** |
| 1 stick celery | 1 lb/500 g medium onions |
| large bouquet garni* | 1 lb/500 g carrots |
| 2 teaspoons peppercorns | 1 lb/500 g turnips |
| 2 lb/1 kg marrow bones | 1 lb/500 g leeks |
| | 1 head celery |

Tie each piece of meat into a neat cylinder with string so it cooks evenly. Tie clove-studded onions, carrots, stick of celery, bouquet garni and peppercorns in cheesecloth. Wrap each marrow bone in muslin so marrow does not fall out.

Put all meat except marrow bones in a very large pot with muslin bag of vegetables, water and salt. Cover and bring slowly to the boil, skimming often. Simmer for about 2 hours, skimming occasionally.

To prepare vegetables: peel onions and halve them. Peel carrots, cut in 3 in/7 cm sticks and tie in bundles. Peel and quarter turnips. Trim leeks, split and wash them thoroughly; tie them in bundles. Peel

outer stalks of celery to remove strings. Cut them in 3 in/7 cm lengths and tie in bundles.

After 2 hours' cooking, add marrow bones to pot with onions and carrots. Simmer 30 minutes more, then add turnips, leeks and celery. Add more water if needed to cover vegetables. Taste broth for seasoning and continue simmering until meats and vegetables are very tender, 30-40 minutes, skimming often. If serving croûtes, toast them.

Lift out meats, marrow bones and vegetables. Boil broth, uncovered, until reduced and well flavoured, 15-20 minutes. Discard strings and arrange vegetables in mounds on a very large serving dish. Set marrow bones at each end. Cover with foil and keep warm.

Discard strings from meats and carve in slices. Arrange slices down centre of dish and keep warm.

Discard muslin bag of vegetables from broth.

Add noodles, if serving, and simmer them until tender, about 5 minutes. Taste broth and spoon into serving bowls. Croûtes should be passed separately. Serve meat and vegetables later as the main course.

### GETTING AHEAD

Cook the pot-au-feu until meats and vegetables are tender. The complete pot-au-feu can be cooked up to 48 hours ahead. Transfer it to a non-metallic bowl to store in the refrigerator. Gently reheat it on top of the stove.

### VARIATION

*Poule au Pot*

Substitute a large casserole hen 6-7 lb/3 kg for meat and marrow bones.

For stuffing: sauté 1 chopped onion in 1 oz/25 g butter until soft. Add 8 oz/250 g finely chopped lean pork and cook, stirring until browned. Take from the heat and stir in 8 oz/250 g finely chopped smoked ham, 1 crushed clove garlic, 2 tablespoons chopped parsley, 2 oz/50 g fresh breadcrumbs and plenty of freshly ground pepper.

Taste and add salt only if necessary. Stuff bird and truss*. Simmer 1/2 hour with bag of vegetables before adding onions and carrots. Then complete as above.

# LEG OF MUTTON POT-AU-FEU WITH GARLIC

## POT-AU-FEU DE GIGOT PROVENÇALE

This recipe is designed for leg of mutton or a very large leg of lamb.

### SERVES 8

| | |
|---|---|
| 6-7 lb/3 kg leg of mutton | salt and pepper |
| 2 cloves garlic, cut in slivers | **For the vegetables** |
| bouquet garni* | 15-20 cloves garlic, peeled |
| 2 teaspoons rosemary | 1 lb/500 g baby onions, peeled |
| 10 peppercorns | |
| 3¼ qt/4 litres water | 1 lb/500 g carrots, peeled and cut into 1 in/2.5 cm chunks |
| toasted croûtes* made with a small loaf of French bread | |

Trim mutton of skin and excess fat (mutton fat is very strong) and tie it tightly with string. Pierce meat with the point of a knife and insert slivers of garlic. Tie bouquet garni, rosemary and peppercorns in muslin.

Put mutton in a large pot with bag of seasonings, water and a little salt. Cover and bring to the boil, skimming often. Simmer until almost tender, 2-3 hours, depending on age of mutton.

If garlic is dry and strong, put whole cloves in a pan of cold water, bring to the boil, simmer 5 minutes and drain. If garlic is fresh, this is not necessary.

After 2-3 hours, add onions, carrots and garlic cloves to mutton. Continue simmering, uncovered, until meat and vegetables are tender, about ¾ hour. Meat is done when it is easily pierced with a two-pronged fork.

Transfer mutton to a serving dish and pile vegetables around it. Cover with foil and keep warm.

Boil broth until reduced and well flavoured, about 10-15 minutes.

Make croûtes.

Taste the broth, and serve it as a first course with the croûtes. Serve mutton and vegetables afterwards as main course.

### GETTING AHEAD

Mutton and vegetables can be completely cooked up to 48 hours ahead. Gently reheat them on top of the stove, then finish as indicated.

### VARIATION

*Beef with Garlic* (Pot-au-feu de bœuf à l'ail)
Substitute a 4½ lb/2¼ kg piece of beef such as brisket or rump for the mutton. Tie beef and simmer until almost tender, 2-3 hours, before adding garlic and vegetables. Finish and serve as mutton.

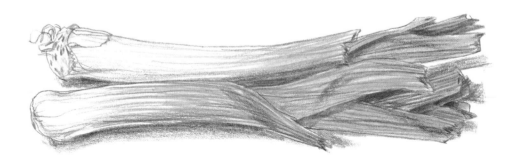

# PORK AND CABBAGE STEW

## POTEE

Potée is a rustic version of pot-au-feu, made with various kinds of pork including ham, bacon and sausages and the most common vegetables – cabbage, carrots, onions, and leeks in season. Often kidney beans or potato are added for bulk. If you can't find garlic sausage for simmering, substitute a piece of gammon.

### SERVES 8

| | |
|---|---|
| 3 lb/1.5 kg ham hock | toasted croûtes* made |
| 2 lb/1 kg piece bacon | with a small loaf of |
| 2 lb/1 kg veal bones | French bread |
| 6½ pts/4 litres water | salt and pepper |
| 10 peppercorns | **For vegetables** |
| 1 clove | 1 lb/500g medium onions |
| bouquet garni* | 1 lb/500 g carrots |
| 1½ lb/750 g garlic | 1 lb/500 g leeks |
| sausage for simmering | 1 medium head cabbage |

Put the ham hock, bacon, veal bones and water in a large pot. Tie peppercorns, clove and bouquet garni in a piece of muslin, add to the pot, cover and bring to the boil, skimming often. Simmer until meats are nearly tender, about 2 hours.

To prepare vegetables: peel onions and halve them. Peel carrots, cut in 3 in/7 cm lengths and tie in bundles. Trim leeks, split, wash them thoroughly and tie in bundles. Discard outer leaves from cabbage, trim stem and cut head into 8 wedges.

After 2 hours' cooking, add onions and carrots to the pot. Taste water, season and simmer 30 minutes more. Add garlic sausage and leeks and continue simmering 15 minutes. Add cabbage and cook until vegetables and meats are tender, 10-15 minutes.

Make croûtes.

Lift out meats and vegetables. Boil broth, uncovered, until reduced and well flavoured, 10-15 minutes. Arrange vegetables, discarding strings, in piles around a large serving dish. Cover with foil and keep warm.

Slice meats and sausage, arrange down the centre of the dish and keep warm.

Discard muslin bag of seasonings and veal bones from broth. Skim excess fat from broth and taste for seasoning. Spoon into serving bowls. Croûtes should be served separately. Serve meat and vegetables later, as the main course.

### GETTING AHEAD

Potée can be cooked completely up to 48 hours ahead. Store it in a non-metallic container in the refrigerator. Gently reheat it on top of the stove.

### VARIATION

*Pork and Cabbage Stew with Potatoes* (Potée d'Auvergne)

To pork and cabbage stew add 2 lb/1 kg potatoes, peeled and halved, with the cabbage.

# 7

# SAVOURY PURÉES AND MOUSSES

In some guise savoury purées and mousses appear in a menu almost everywhere. Meat and fish mousses are a a classic first course or they can form a main dish according to your taste. Vegetable purées may accompany a main course or, with hollandaise or a cream sauce, they can be served as a light opening to a meal. Purées and mousses suit the prettiness of the new individual plate presentations.

### PUREES

To purée a vegetable requires little more skill than to boil it. Indeed most purées *are* boiled vegetables, which have been finely mashed or sieved, then enriched with butter and cream. The vegetables should be cooked slightly longer than usual, so they can be puréed easily. The food processor is a boon in puréeing most ingredients, and a blender is worth trying for soft vegetables like tomatoes. Otherwise hand labour is needed with a mouli vegetable mill, a traditional drum sieve and 'mushroom' pestle, or simply with a bowl strainer and a wooden spoon. The simplest way to obtain a purée is with a masher. Although usually limited to puréeing potatoes and other root vegetables, a masher has the advantage that it can be used in the cooking pan. Vegetable mills and sieves are good for removing skin (as in peas) or strings (as in celery). For really smooth results it is sometimes necessary to push a

purée through a sieve by hand after working it in an electric processor or blender.

The finishing touches to purées are given on reheating. If too wet (often the case with pumpkin or greens like spinach), a purée should be cooked gently over the heat with butter until it dries to the appropriate consistency – usually when it just falls easily from the spoon. Soft purées, such as tomato, can be further stiffened by beating in whipped egg white, which technically speaking transforms them into a mousse. If, on the other hand, a purée is sticky because of the starch content – common with dried beans and chestnuts – it should be thinned with liquid from cooking, or with cream.

All purées must be stirred constantly during reheating, but do not beat vigorously; in fact vegetables such as potatoes with a high starch content become elastic if overworked (for this reason, they should not be puréed in the food processor). The seasoning of purées is a delicate matter too. Plenty of salt and pepper are needed, butter enhances most vegetables and cream enriches greens, particularly acid ones such as sorrel. Like most French chefs, I'm a partisan of nutmeg, and with wintry purées like chestnut or lentil, you can go further and add allspice and cloves. Taste the purée as you blend it.

A vegetable purée is the perfect accompaniment to

many main courses; classic combinations include chestnut purée with game, spinach with ham, mushroom with chicken. One agreeable custom is to serve two, or even three, contrasting purées with the same dish. Sometimes a vegetable purée is moulded by mixing it with eggs and white sauce (p. 10) or breadcrumbs, then baking it in a timbale or ramekin. Often the mould is lined with spinach leaves so the contents are a surprise and the vegetables may be set in multicoloured layers. These little castles of carrot or spinach make a charming garnish for main courses.

### MOUSSES AND MOUSSELINES

Mousse is a very general term, simply meaning 'foam'. The same standards apply to mousses as to purées, whether they be made of meat, fish or vegetable. The flavour should be definite, and the consistency soft but not wet. Most important for a mousse is a fine texture, obtained only by prolonged working in a food processor or by rubbing through a drum sieve. As with purées, the main ingredient is cooked first, but then it is mixed with whipped cream, egg white, or some other ingredient which will lighten it.

The type of mousse called a mousseline is more specific – it is always made with raw meat (usually chicken, veal or fish) that is puréed, bound with egg white and enriched with cream. The mixture is packed in a mould and cooked in a water bath. Mousselines need a rich butter sauce (pp. 18-19), and they are remarkable for their fine texture and intense flavour.

### QUENELLES

The last member of the mousse family is quenelles, dumplings which are made on the same principle as mousselines, but bound with a thick paste (panade) of butter, flour and milk or water. Eggs are also included, so that the finished quenelles are not only more substantial, but also more open-textured than a mousseline. Quenelle mixture can be baked in a mould, as in turban of sole, but more often it is shaped into ovals with two spoons and poached in salted water or stock before serving in a sauce.

# PUREE OF CELERIAC

## PUREE DE CELERI-RAVE

Being low in gluten, celeriac is always combined with some potato when it is puréed to give it body.

---

### SERVES 4-6

| | |
|---|---|
| 1½ lb/750 g celeriac | pinch of sugar |
| juice of ½ lemon | 4 fl oz/125 ml milk, more |
| 2 medium potatoes | if needed |
| 1½ oz/40 g butter | salt and pepper |

---

Peel celeriac, cut it in ½ in/1 cm slices and at once immerse it in a saucepan of cold salted water with lemon juice. Once cut, celeriac discolours quickly. Cover pan and simmer until celeriac is tender, 20-25 minutes. Peel potatoes, cut them in 2-3 chunks and add to celeriac. Continue cooking until vegetables are tender, 15-20 minutes.

Drain vegetables and mash them or work them through a food mill or drum sieve. Do not use a food processor as the purée will become elastic and fibres in the celeriac will not be reduced to a purée.

Return purée to the pan with butter, sugar, some of the milk, salt and pepper. Heat, beating constantly, until the purée is light. Heat expands starch grains in the purée, making it white and fluffy. Add more milk, salt and pepper if necessary to taste.

### GETTING AHEAD

Celeriac purée is best served at once, but it can be kept 24 hours if the surface is smoothed and covered with a thin layer of milk. Keep purée in the refrigerator and, just before serving, beat milk into the purée. Reheat gently.

### VARIATIONS

*Cauliflower Purée* (Purée de chou-fleur)
Substitute a large cauliflower for celeriac and use only the florets. Boil potatoes 10 minutes, add

cauliflower and continue cooking together until tender, 5-7 minutes.

*Turnip Purée (Purée de navets)*
Substitute turnips for celeriac. Boil the turnips 5-10 minutes before adding potatoes.

# PUREE OF GREEN PEAS

## PUREE DE PETITS POIS

This purée is excellent made with fresh peas and surprisingly good made with frozen ones.

### SERVES 4

| | |
|---|---|
| 1 lb/500 g shelled fresh peas | 2 tablespoons double cream |
| salt and pepper | 1 tablespoon chopped fresh mint, or more to taste |
| 1 oz/25 g butter | |

Bring a large pan of salted water to the boil. Add peas and cook in boiling water, 10-25 minutes, depending on age.

Drain peas and rinse with cold water to set their colour. Drain thoroughly and purée in a food processor or work through a vegetable mill.

Heat butter in a saucepan and cook purée, stirring, until very hot. Add cream; the purée should be just thick enough to fall from the spoon. If too thick, add more cream and if too thin, keep cooking until moisture evaporates. Taste purée for seasoning, stir in mint and serve at once.

### GETTING AHEAD
Pea purée is best served at once, though it can be kept 48 hours in the refrigerator. Reheat it in butter and add cream just before serving.

### VARIATION
*Green Bean Purée (Purée de haricots verts)*
Substitute green beans for peas and omit mint. Top and tail beans and cook in boiling water until tender, 8-15 minutes, depending on size.

# SPINACH AND CARROT RAMEKINS

## TIMBALES D'EPINARDS ET CAROTTES

These vegetable ramekins are a pleasant accompaniment to most fish, poultry and meat dishes. When served with hollandaise sauce they can also be used as a first course.

### SERVES 6

| | |
|---|---|
| 2 lb/1 kg fresh spinach | ¾ pt/450 ml thick white sauce (p. 10) |
| salt and pepper | 4 eggs, beaten to mix |
| 1 oz/25 g butter | pinch of grated nutmeg |
| 1 lb/500 g carrots, peeled and sliced | 8 fl oz/250 ml hollandaise sauce (p. 19) (optional) |

Wash spinach well, discard stalks and reserve 24-30 large leaves. Bring a large pan of salted water to the boil. Add large leaves and boil until limp, 1-2 minutes. Drain on paper towels and reserve. Add remaining spinach to pan and boil until tender, about 5 minutes. Drain, squeeze with your hands to remove excess water and chop finely.

In a saucepan heat half the butter and cook the spinach, stirring, until very dry, 3-4 minutes.

Put carrots in a pan of salted water, cover and bring to the boil. Simmer until tender, 10-15 minutes. Drain thoroughly. Purée in a food processor or blender or work through a vegetable mill. Heat remaining butter in a saucepan and cook carrot purée, stirring, until water evaporates and it is stiff enough to hold a shape. Let it cool.

Set oven at 180°C/350°F/gas 4. Butter ramekins of 4 fl oz/125 ml capacity and line them with large spinach leaves.

Make thick white sauce and stir half into the spinach. Add half of the beaten eggs. Add nutmeg and taste for seasoning. Spoon mixture into the ramekins to half fill them. Add remaining white sauce to carrots and stir in remaining eggs. Taste for seasoning. Fill ramekins with rest of the carrot mixture. Cook ramekins in a water bath* until mixture is firm, 20-30 minutes.

Make hollandaise, if serving, and keep warm in water bath on top of stove.

To unmould: lift ramekins from water bath and let cool slightly. Run a knife around edge of the mixture and turn moulds onto individual plates. Spoon hollandaise sauce around the moulds if serving as a first course.

### GETTING AHEAD

Moulds can be kept warm in a water bath for up to 30 minutes. They can also be cooked ahead and refrigerated for up to 36 hours; reheat them in a water bath on top of the stove.

### VARIATION

*Cauliflower and Spinach Ramekins* (Timbales d'épinards et chou-fleur)
Substitute a medium head of cauliflower for the carrots. Cook florets in boiling salted water until tender, about 5 minutes. Drain thoroughly, purée and dry in butter as for carrots.

---

# HOT TOMATO MOUSSE

## MOUSSE DE TOMATE CHAUDE

Serve this mousse with grilled or roast poultry or fish.

---

### SERVES 8

| | |
|---|---|
| 2 tablespoons olive oil | large bouquet garni* |
| 1 onion, finely chopped | salt and pepper |
| 4 lb/2 kg ripe tomatoes, peeled, seeded and chopped* | pinch of sugar (optional) |
| | 3 egg whites |
| 2 cloves garlic, crushed | |

---

In a large sauté pan heat oil and cook onion until soft but not brown, 5-7 minutes. Add tomatoes, garlic, bouquet garni, salt and pepper and cook over medium heat, stirring often, until mixture is thick enough to hold a shape, 20-30 minutes depending on juiciness of the tomatoes.

Discard bouquet garni and purée tomatoes in a food processor or blender. Taste for seasoning, adding sugar if tomatoes are acid. Return to a saucepan and keep warm.

Stiffly beat the egg whites. Whisk egg whites, a little at a time, into hot tomato purée. Vigorous whisking is important so egg whites thicken the mixture without formation of lumps. Taste for seasoning.

### GETTING AHEAD

Tomato purée can be refrigerated for 48 hours. Add egg whites when reheating.
The finished mousse can be kept hot in a water bath* for up to 30 minutes if necessary.

### VARIATION

*Hot Tomato Mousse with Herbs* (Mousse de tomate chaude aux herbes)
Before serving, stir in 2 tablespoons chopped fresh basil, oregano, chives or mint. Do not use dried herbs.

# HOT TURBAN MOULD OF SALMON

## TURBAN DE SAUMON

The salmon mousse can also be cooked alone, without the sole fillets.

---

### SERVES 6

**For panade**

1/4 pt/150 ml milk

2 oz/50 g butter

2 oz/50 g flour

**For salmon mousse**

3/4 lb/375 g piece of salmon

3/4 lb/375 g sole fillets, with the bones

2 egg whites, beaten to mix

6 fl oz/175 ml crème fraîche* **or** double cream

salt and white pepper

6-8 large cooked prawns

**For tomato sauce (sauce aurore)**

1 1/2 oz/40 g butter

3 tablespoons flour

3/4 pt/450 ml fish stock* made with sole and salmon bones

4 fl oz/125 ml crème fraîche* **or** double cream

1-2 tablespoons tomato purée

---

For the panade: in a saucepan bring milk and butter just to the boil. Take from heat and add flour all at once. Beat vigorously with a wooden spoon until panade is smooth and pulls away from sides of pan. Return to heat and cook, beating constantly, until it forms a ball, 2-3 minutes. Leave to cool.

Cut bone from salmon, then cut away skin and discard it. Make fish stock* using the sole and salmon bones.

To make salmon mousse: cut salmon flesh in pieces and purée in a food processor until smooth. Gradually add egg whites, followed by cooled panade, and continue working in processor until smooth. Alternatively, work salmon, egg whites and panade a little at a time in a blender. Transfer mixture to a metal bowl and set it over ice. Beat in cream, a little at a time with salt and pepper; taste for seasoning. Chill mousse until very cold and stiff, 15-30 minutes.

Set oven at 180°C/350°F/gas 4. Butter a 2 1/2 pt/ 1.5 litre ring mould. Cut sole fillets in half lengthwise and line mould with them, setting them skinned side up, and letting broad end of fillet hang over outer rim of mould, with tapered end over inner rim. Space fillets evenly, leaving v-shaped gaps between them. Spoon salmon mixture into mould and fold fillet ends on top. Cover mould with buttered foil and cook in a water bath* until turban is firm to the touch, 35-45 minutes.

Make tomato sauce: in a saucepan melt the butter over medium heat. Whisk in flour and cook until foaming. Add fish stock and bring to the boil, whisking until sauce thickens. Season lightly and simmer 2 minutes. Stir in cream and just enough tomato purée to colour sauce a deep pink. Simmer 2 more minutes and taste for seasoning.

Remove mould from water bath and let cool slightly. Pour boiling water over shrimps; leave until hot, about 1 minute, and drain them.

To finish: tip excess liquid from side of mould and turn turban out onto a round serving dish. Wipe away any liquid and coat turban and dish with tomato sauce. Set shrimps around the dish, or on top of turban, and serve any remaining sauce separately.

### GETTING AHEAD

Turban and sauce can be cooked up to 8 hours ahead and refrigerated. While sauce is still hot, rub the surface with butter to prevent a skin forming. Reheat mould in a water bath* for 15-20 minutes on top of stove. Reheat sauce on top of stove.

### VARIATION

*Hot Salmon Mousse* (Mousse de saumon)
Omit sole and tomato sauce. Put the mousse mixture into a 1 3/4 pt/1 litre charlotte mould, or into 6 individual ramekin moulds. Cook in a water bath* until firm, 35-45 minutes for the charlotte mould, or 20-25 minutes for individual moulds. Serve with hollandaise or white butter sauce (p. 19).

# —8—
# PATES AND TERRINES

Pâtés and terrines are a mainstay of the French table. Standard opening to a family lunch is pork terrine or pâté of duck, both surprisingly inexpensive when bought from the local charcuterie. More luxurious are fish pâtés, and the vegetable terrines arranged in layers, so that when sliced they display a pretty mosaic pattern typical of nouvelle cuisine.

Strictly speaking, a terrine should always be baked in a terrine mould (traditionally made of earthenware), while a pâté should be considered to be enclosed in pastry – pâté. Nowadays, the difference is blurred and a pâté often appears in the form of a terrine, or packed into a mould without a pastry crust. The point is that pâtés and terrines are judged by the same criteria. Texture is important: a terrine should be coarse and a pâté smooth and silky. Some pâtés, such as cheese herb pâté, are naturally smooth, but most need to be puréed in a blender (for soft mixtures) or a food processor (for firmer fish, poultry and meats). Failing machines, a good deal of elbow-grease is needed to work a pâté through the traditional drum sieve. Terrines should not have the fine texture of a pâté, so the meat is minced. A food processor can be used, but a mincer is better as it cuts rather than pounds the meat. If the terrine mixture is overworked it will be tough when cooked.

Both pâtés and terrines should have a careful balance of flavours. The main ingredient – for example, smoked salmon, pheasant or pork – must be enriched with fat. For pâtés this may be butter or cream; for terrines it is invariably pork fat. There are many possible flavourings, like onion, garlic, bacon and wine, while eggs bind the mixture and brandy helps storage. Seasoning must be carefully judged – better a spicy result than a tasteless one. For baked mixtures, a small piece must be sautéed and tasted: it should be strong, for the seasonings will mellow when cooked in the oven. All moulds should be lined with pork fat or bacon to protect the contents against the heat of the oven.

To prevent flavour from escaping, a tight-fitting lid is usually indispensable when cooking a moulded pâté or terrine. However country versions are sometimes baked uncovered, and develop a crusty brown top which compensates for the loss of flavour. Covered or uncovered, the mould should be completely filled, as the mixture will shrink a bit in the oven. The mould is placed in a water bath* and cooked in a moderate oven so the heat penetrates slowly to the centre.

Here's where the skewer* test to see if the mixture is done is vital: fish and pork pâtés and terrines must be piping hot at the centre, while duck and game varieties should be just hot, so they stay juicy and slightly pink. After cooking, leave the mixture in the mould until tepid, then uncover it and press the top with weights of a couple of pounds or a kilo; a brick is handy for this since it will compress the mixture for easy slicing without squeezing out the juices.

Eye appeal is part of the charm of a pâté or terrine, with

its marbled decoration formed by laying strips of meat or fish or vegetables lengthwise in the mould, so they are sliced crosswise for serving. Other easy ways to add colour to terrine mixtures are by adding a handful of pistachio nuts, toasted hazelnuts, or the extravagance of a chopped truffle or two.

Bread is obligatory with meat terrines – whole wheat, country bread or French baguette – while hot toast is best with creamy pâtés. By contrast, fish and vegetable terrines should be served with an appropriate sauce. They may be hot or cold, and can form a light main dish or a first course.

Pâtés and terrines keep well – indeed, they benefit from storage as the flavours mellow. Pâtés packed in a container can be safely refrigerated a day or two, while pâtés and terrines baked in a mould can be stored in the refrigerator, from 3 days for vegetables and fish mixtures, to a week or more for pork and game terrines that have been cooked with brandy. Storage time is doubled by sealing the surface with melted fat, either clarified butter for delicate pâtés, or lard for game and meat terrines. Once cut, however, pâtés and terrines should be eaten within 2 or 3 days.

# SMOKED SALMON PATE

## PATE DE SAUMON FUME

For this recipe, inexpensive trimmings of smoked salmon can be used.

### SERVES 4

| | |
|---|---|
| 6 oz/175 g smoked salmon | freshly ground black pepper |
| 2 oz/50 g butter, softened | salt |
| 4 fl oz/125 ml crème fraîche **or** double cream | ½ lemon, thinly sliced, **or** several sprigs of parsley (for decoration) |
| juice of ½ lemon | |
| cayenne pepper | |

Purée salmon in a food processor or blender until very smooth and creamy.

Beat in butter and cream a little at a time. Season to taste with lemon juice, cayenne and pepper; salt

may not be necessary as the salmon is already salty.

Pack pâté into individual ramekins or into a crock and chill. Just before serving, decorate it with lemon slices or parsley sprigs. Serve the pâté at room temperature.

### GETTING AHEAD
The pâté can be made 2-3 days ahead and refrigerated. Leave it at room temperature for about 1 hour before serving.
### VARIATION
*Smoked Trout Pâté (Pâté de truite fumée)*
Substitute ½ lb/250 g boned and flaked smoked trout for the smoked salmon. Season highly with grated or creamed horseradish, lemon juice and a pinch of cayenne.

# CHICKEN LIVER AND APPLE PATE

## PATE DE FOIES DE VOLAILLES NORMANDE

The tartness of apple combines well with the richness of chicken liver.

### SERVES 6-8

| | |
|---|---|
| 1 lb/500 g chicken livers | 4 fl oz/125 ml red wine |
| 1 lb/500 g bacon rashers | 2 sprigs parsley |
| 1 tart apple, peeled, cored and chopped | salt and pepper |
| 1 onion, chopped | 1 oz/25 g clarified butter* |

Roughly chop liver and bacon. Put them in a sauté pan with the chopped apple, onion, wine and parsley. Cover and cook gently 30 minutes. Leave to cool.

Purée mixture in a food processor or blender until very smooth and creamy. Season to taste with pepper; salt may not be needed if the bacon is very salty.

Spoon the pâté into individual ramekins or into

a crock and smooth the top. Chill until set, 1-2 hours. Carefully pour clarified butter over pâté to seal it from the air so it does not discolour. The flavour mellows if the pâté is kept at least 24 hours. Serve it chilled.

### VARIATION

*Chicken Liver and Apple Pâté with Walnuts* (Pâté de foies de volailles normande aux noix)
After puréeing chicken liver and apple pâté, stir in 2 oz/50 g coarsely chopped walnuts. Decorate each ramekin with a walnut half.

## COUNTRY PORK PATE

### PATE DE CAMPAGNE

This smooth pâté is puréed in a food processor but, for a rougher texture, the minced meats may be simply mixed in a bowl.

### SERVES 8-10

| | |
|---|---|
| 1 tablespoon butter | 2 cloves garlic, peeled |
| 1 onion, chopped | ½ teaspoon ground allspice |
| ½ lb/250 g minced lean pork | |
| | pinch of ground cloves |
| ½ lb/250 g minced pork fat | pinch of ground nutmeg |
| | 2 eggs, beaten to mix |
| ½ lb/250 g minced veal | 2 tablespoons brandy |
| ½ lb/250 g pork or chicken liver, finely chopped | salt and pepper |
| | ½ lb/250 g bacon rashers |

Melt butter in a small sauté pan and cook onion over low heat until soft but not brown, 10-15 minutes. Leave to cool.

In a food processor, purée the pork, pork fat, veal, pork or chicken liver, garlic, allspice, cloves, nutmeg, eggs, cooked onion, brandy, salt and pepper. Divide the mixture in half if it does not all fit comfortably in the machine. Sauté a small piece of mixture and taste for seasoning. It should be highly seasoned; if not, add more salt and pepper.

Set oven at 180°C/350°F/gas 4. Line the sides and the base of a ¾ pt/1 litre terrine mould with bacon, reserving 2 rashers. Pack pork mixture in the mould and smooth the top. Cut remaining bacon in thin strips and arrange in a lattice on top of the pâté.

Cook the pâté, uncovered, in a water bath* until done when tested with a skewer*, 1¼-1½ hours. Let pâté cool to tepid.

Remove lid and insert a board that fits inside the rim. Distribute weights on top and chill. Serve pâté from the mould and cut it in slices at the table.

### GETTING AHEAD

The pâté should be made at least 48 hours ahead so that flavours mellow. It can be kept up to 5 days in the refrigerator.

### VARIATIONS

*Pork Pâté with Hazelnuts* (Pâté de porc solognote)
Add 4 oz/125 g toasted peeled hazelnuts to the pork mixture.

*Marbled Pork Pâté* (Pâté de porc marbré)
Roll each chicken liver in very thinly sliced pork fat or fat bacon. Make pâté mixture without livers. Pack half mixture into mould and place livers down the centre. Cover with the remaining mixture and bake. When sliced, the pâté is marbled with liver outlined with fat.

# MOSAIC TERRINE OF VEGETABLES

## MOSAIQUE DE LEGUMES

This terrine earns its name from the colourful pattern of vegetables, arranged in layers and bound with a batter resembling that used for crêpes.

---

### SERVES 8-10

**For batter**

3 oz/75 g flour

5 eggs

8 fl oz/250 ml milk

2 oz/50 g chopped chives or parsley

pinch of cayenne

salt

**For vegetables**

1 lb/500 g carrots, peeled and cut lengthwise into thin slices

1 medium cauliflower, divided into florets

¾ lb/375 g fresh green beans

1 lb/500 g fresh spinach

1 tablespoon butter

**For serving**

¼ pt/150 ml tomato mayonnaise (p. 17)

¼ pt/150 ml chantilly mayonnaise (p. 17)

---

For the batter: sift flour into a bowl and make a well in the centre. Add eggs and whisk, gradually drawing in flour to make a smooth batter. Stir in milk with herbs, cayenne and salt to taste. The batter should be highly seasoned. Cover and leave to rest at least 1 hour.

To cook vegetables: cook each vegetable separately, in a large quantity of boiling salted water, until just tender.

Allow 5-6 minutes for cauliflower and carrots, 4-8 minutes for the green beans, depending on their size – and drain. Rinse green beans with cold water and drain again.

For spinach, remove the stems and wash leaves thoroughly. Cook 1-2 minutes in a large pan of boiling salted water. Drain and rinse with cold water. Squeeze the leaves to remove excess water.

Set oven at 180°C/350°F/gas 4. Thickly butter a 2 pt/1.25 litre terrine mould.

To fill terrine: stir batter and pour a ½ in/1.5 cm layer into mould. Pack a tightly fitting layer of cauliflower pieces in bottom of mould and spoon in a little more of the batter. Cover with a single layer of spinach. Place carrot sticks lengthwise and moisten again with batter. Repeat process with spinach, green beans, and cauliflower.

Pour remaining batter into mould so vegetables are just covered, inserting a skewer every few inches to allow batter to seep through.

Cover mould with buttered foil, allowing room for the batter to rise. Cook the terrine in a water bath* until done when tested with a skewer* – 1-1¼ hours. This terrine must be very thoroughly cooked or it will fall apart when unmoulded. Let terrine cool, then chill it in refrigerator.

Be sure terrine is thoroughly chilled before unmoulding. Plunge mould into boiling water for 1 minute, run a knife around edges of custard and unmould onto a board.

Cut terrine into thick slices.

To serve: coat individual plates with tomato mayonnaise at one side and chantilly mayonnaise (p. 17) at the other. Set one or two slices of terrine on each plate, on top of the mayonnaise.

### GETTING AHEAD

Vegetable terrine is best made at least 12 hours ahead so it chills thoroughly. It can be kept up to 3 days in the refrigerator.

### VARIATION

*Mosaic Terrine of Green Vegetables* (Mosaique de légumes verts)
Substitute fresh asparagus for carrots, and broccoli florets for cauliflower.

Trim and peel asparagus and cook in boiling salted water until almost tender, 8-10 minutes. Cook broccoli as for cauliflower.

Sorrel may be substituted for spinach, or use half spinach and half sorrel, combining the sharpness of the sorrel with the firm texture of the spinach.

# TERRINE OF HAM

## TERRINE DE JAMBON

Simple boiled ham, which is not too salty, is best for this terrine.

### SERVES 10-12

| | |
|---|---|
| 1 tablespoon butter | 2 eggs, beaten to mix |
| 2 onions, finely chopped | 3 tablespoons brandy |
| 1¼ lb/625 g pork liver, finely chopped | salt and pepper |
| 1¼ lb/625 g minced pork, half fat and half lean | ¾ lb/375 g bacon rashers |
| | 4 chicken livers |
| 1 clove garlic, crushed | ¾ lb/375 g cooked ham, cut into thick strips |
| 2 tablespoons chopped parsley | 1 bay leaf |
| | 20-24 pickled gherkins |

Melt butter in a small sauté pan. Add onion and cook until soft but not browned; let cool. In a large bowl, combine pork liver, pork, garlic, parsley, onion, eggs, brandy, salt and pepper. Mix until seasoning is evenly blended. Sauté a small piece of mixture and taste for seasoning; it should be highly seasoned.

Set oven at 180°C/350°F/gas 4. Line the bottom of terrine mould with a few rashers of bacon. Wrap a strip of bacon around each chicken liver and reserve the rest. Spread a quarter of the pork mixture in the mould and lay half the ham strips on top. Cover with one quarter more pork and set chicken livers on top. Add half remaining pork mixture, followed by a layer of ham, and then the rest of the pork. Top terrine with remaining bacon, add the bay leaf and cover with the lid.

Cook the terrine in a water bath* until done when tested with a skewer*, 1¼-1½ hours.

Let terrine cool to tepid. Remove lid and press terrine with a board or plate that fits just inside the rim; distribute weights on top and chill.

To serve: run a knife around the sides of the terrine and turn onto a board. Cut terrine into slices and arrange them, overlapping, on a serving dish or on individual plates. To decorate, slice gherkins lengthwise in three, leaving top attached, and press open to create a fan effect. Set fans on terrine.

### GETTING AHEAD
Make ham terrine at least 48 hours ahead so that flavours mellow. It can be refrigerated for up to 5 days.

### VARIATIONS
*Pork Liver Pâté* (Pâté de foie de porc)
Omit ham and chicken livers and use all the bacon for lining terrine.
*Veal and Ham Terrine* (Terrine de veau et de jambon)
Substitute minced lean veal for the pork liver.

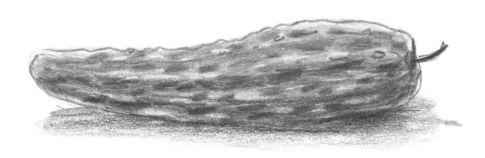

# TERRINE OF PHEASANT

## TERRINE DE FAISAN

A terrine is an excellent end for an old game bird, which would be tough if roasted in the oven.

---

### SERVES 8

| | |
|---|---|
| 1 large pheasant, with the giblets | 1 clove garlic, crushed |
| 1/4 lb/125 g uncooked ham, cut into strips | 1/4 teaspoon of ground allspice |
| 1/4 lb/125 g pork back fat, cut into strips | pinch of ground cloves |
| 3 tablespoons brandy | pinch of ground nutmeg |
| 3 tablespoons Madeira | 2 eggs, beaten to mix |
| 3/4 lb/375 g bacon rashers | salt and pepper |
| 1 lb/500 g minced pork, half fat, half lean | 1 bay leaf |
| | a few juniper berries (optional) |

---

With a sharp pointed knife, cut all meat from pheasant carcass. Discard skin. Cut breast meat into strips. Scrape sinews from leg meat. Put breast meat with ham and pork strips, pour brandy and Madeira over them, cover and leave to marinate*.

Finely chop 2 rashers of bacon and sauté until the fat runs. Add liver and heart from pheasant and sauté until brown but still pink in the centre, about 5 minutes. Let mixture cool.

Work pheasant leg meat and any trimmings

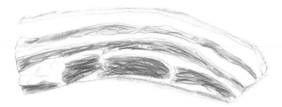

through the mincer with the liver mixture and both the lean and fat pork. Mix in garlic, allspice, cloves, nutmeg, eggs, salt and pepper. Add marinade from meat strips and beat until seasoning is evenly blended. Cook a small piece of mixture in frying pan and taste; it should be quite spicy. If not, add more seasoning.

Set oven at 180°C/350°F/gas 4. Line the base and the sides of a 2½ pt/1.5 litre terrine mould with bacon, reserving 1 or 2 rashers. Spread a quarter of the pork mixture on the bottom and lay half the ham and pork fat strips on top. Cover with another quarter of the pork mixture and add a layer of pheasant strips. Top with half the remaining pork, followed by remaining ham and pork back fat strips and then the rest of the pork. Cover with the reserved bacon. Set the bay leaf on top, and, if using, the juniper berries. Add the lid.

Cook the terrine in a water bath* until done when tested with a skewer; 1¼-1½ hours. Let terrine cool to tepid. Remove lid and set a board just inside the rim of the terrine; distribute weights on the board and chill.

To serve: run a knife along the sides of the terrine, unmould it onto a board and cut it into slices, or serve it from the mould.

### GETTING AHEAD

Pheasant terrine should be made at least 48 hours ahead so the flavour mellows. It can be kept up to a week in the refrigerator.

### VARIATIONS

*Duck Terrine* (Terrine de canard)
Substitute a duck for the pheasant. Strip the skin from the duck in one piece if possible and use it to line the terrine mould.

*Game Terrine* (Terrine de gibier)
Omit pheasant and substitute 1 lb/500 g trimmed meat of any game such as venison, wild duck or hare.

*Rabbit Terrine* (Terrine de lapin)
Substitute a medium rabbit for the pheasant. Cut meat from bones of rabbit. Cut saddle in strips and marinate as for pheasant breast. Mince leg meat with liver and pork.

# HOT TERRINE OF SEAFOOD

## TERRINE DE FRUITS DE MER

Almost all fish terrines are made of a mousseline mixture (p. 56) which is baked in a terrine mould. This particular recipe can be served hot, with a white butter sauce (p. 19), or cold with green or tomato mayonnaise (p. 17).

### SERVES 8-10

| | |
|---|---|
| 1¾ pt/1 litre mussels, cleaned, cooked and shelled* | flounder fillets |
| ¾ lb/375 g cooked shelled shrimps, diced | ½ lb/250 g cooked shelled shrimps |
| ¼ lb/125 g shelled scallops*, diced | 2½ oz/65 g butter |
| 1 tablespoon butter | salt and pepper |
| **For seafood mousseline** | 1 egg, separated |
| 1 lb/500 g shelled scallops* | 8 fl oz/250 ml crème fraîche* or double cream |
| ¾ lb/375 g whiting or | cayenne |
| | **To serve** |
| | 8 fl oz/250 ml white butter sauce (p. 19) |

Prepare the mussels and chill.

For the mousseline: purée scallops, whiting or flounder fillets and shrimps in a food processor. Work in butter with a pinch of salt, followed by the egg yolk. Transfer mixture to a metal bowl and set it over ice. Using a wooden spoon, beat in egg white, and then the cream, adding it a few tablespoons at a time. Beat the mixture over ice so it is thoroughly chilled. It should be quite stiff, but if soft, refrigerate it for half an hour. Season it to taste with cayenne, salt and pepper.

Set oven at 180°C/350°F/gas 4. Butter a 3¼ pt/2 litre terrine mould. Beat the diced shrimp and scallops into the mousseline mixture. Stir in the mussels. Fill mould with mixture, packing it down well, and cover the terrine with a lid.

Cook terrine in a water bath* until done when tested with a skewer*, 1½-1¾ hours.

When the terrine is cooked, leave it to stand in the water bath for 10-15 minutes.

Make the white butter sauce.

To unmould terrine: run a knife around the edge of the mixture and turn onto a board. Cut terrine into slices.

To serve: set one or two slices of terrine on individual plates and spoon sauce around the edge.

### GETTING AHEAD

Seafood terrine can be cooked 48 hours ahead and refrigerated. Reheat it in a water bath* and make the sauce at the last minute. Alternatively serve it cold with green mayonnaise.

### VARIATION

*Hot Fish Terrine* (Terrine de poisson)
Omit the diced shellfish and make the mousseline mixture with 3 lb/1.5 kg whiting, flounder or other white fish fillets. Add colour to the mousseline by stirring in ½ green pepper and ½ red pepper, which have been cored, diced and cooked in boiling water until just tender, 1-2 minutes, and then drained.

# 9
# CREPES

Pancake is no translation for crêpe. I remember with nostalgia the thick butter fried pancakes of my childhood, which I ate dripping with golden syrup, but they bear no more relation to lacy French crêpes than do hearty American breakfast pancakes raised with baking powder.

A crêpe acts as a container for mixtures which are rolled or folded inside. Light in texture and unobtrusive in flavour, the crêpe should form a background to the filling. This can vary from sweet to savoury, from white sauce with a sprinkling of cheese to substantial combinations of shellfish with mushrooms or chicken in a cream sauce.

The batter for most crêpes is plain, made of white flour, eggs, milk, salt and a tablespoon or two of melted butter. For a nutty flavour, whole wheat or buckwheat flour can be substituted for a portion of the plain flour. A more substantial change is to put a flavour like sweet corn or a purée of green beans or spinach directly into the batter in place of the traditional filling. These flavoured crêpes provide an attractive and unusual accompaniment for both poultry and meat.

The ideal, wafer thin texture of a crêpe depends on three things: how the batter is mixed, its consistency, and the pan in which it is cooked.

The standard crêpe pan is made of heavy iron, but a non-stick surface is good too. The diameter of the pan can vary; 7 in/18 cm is a good average. The sides should be shallow so that the pan is light and easy to control. When new, iron pans need to be proved*, thereafter they should never be washed, but simply wiped out with a clean cloth after use.

When mixing, batter should be whisked only until smooth, so gluten in the flour is not developed to toughen the finished crêpe. To avoid lumps, make a well in the flour, add half the milk and stir just until mixed; then the eggs and the remaining milk can be added without any problem. In any case, a lump or two is of no consequence – simply pour the batter through a strainer.

After mixing, the batter is left to stand at least an hour; it will thicken as the grains of starch in the flour absorb the milk. The final consistency should be that of thin cream. The best way to test is to fry an experimental crêpe or two. If they are heavy, thin the batter with more milk. If the batter is too thin, whisk in an egg. Thickening the batter with more flour is difficult and not recommended.

For frying crêpes, there is no substitute for butter. Oil or margarine can be used, but they will give neither the same golden colour nor the rich flavour. To lessen scorching, the butter should be clarified*. Before you begin frying, assemble a ladle for the batter, a metal spatula to turn the crêpes and a plate to receive them. Prepare the pan by heating a generous amount of clarified butter, then pour it out to use later. (The pan will need buttering after frying half a dozen crêpes.) Quickly add a small ladle of batter, revolving the pan with a turn of the wrist so the base is completely coated. With too much batter the crêpe will

be heavy, but with too little it will have holes.

Fry the crêpe quickly over quite high heat until set on top and brown underneath, then turn it and brown the other side. The underside of the crêpe cooks more evenly and looks more attractive so make sure it is on the outside when the crêpe is folded. Tossing crêpes is fun, and easy with a non-stick pan, but really quite unnecessary – chefs call it 'du cinéma'. When cooked, the crêpes should be piled one on another to keep warm and moist.

The first crêpe of the batch often sticks, even in a well-proved pan, so don't hesitate to discard it. After 1 or 2 tries you'll have gauged the consistency of the batter and the right amount to add to the pan. Then away you go: a crêpe every 30 seconds is an average output, and after a while you'll be able to keep 2 or even 3 pans going at once.

---

# CREPES

## CREPES

The batter for crêpes can be made with only plain flour, or with the mixture of half plain, half whole wheat suggested here, which gives a more robust, nutty flavour.

### MAKES 14-16 CREPES

| | |
|---|---|
| 2 oz/50 g plain flour | 3 eggs |
| 2 oz/50 g whole wheat flour | 1 oz/25 g melted butter |
| ¼ teaspoon salt | 2 oz/50 g clarified butter*, more if needed |
| 8 fl oz/250 ml milk, more if needed | |

For the batter: sift plain flour into a large bowl and stir in whole wheat flour. Make a well in centre of flour and add salt and half the milk. Whisk to make a smooth mixture. Whisk in eggs; do not overbeat or batter will become elastic and crêpes will be tough. Stir in melted butter with half remaining milk. Cover and let batter stand 1-2 hours; it will thicken slightly.

To fry crêpes: stir in remaining milk, adding

more if needed, to make a batter the consistency of thin cream. Brush crêpe pan with clarified butter or oil. Heat until a drop of batter sprinkled in the pan sizzles. Pour 2-3 tablespoons batter into pan, turning quickly to coat bottom evenly. Cook over medium-high heat until crêpe is browned on the bottom. Turn with a metal spatula, brown the other side and turn out onto a plate.

Continue with remaining batter, buttering pan only when crêpes start to stick. Pile cooked crêpes on top of each other to keep bottom ones moist and warm.

### GETTING AHEAD

Crêpe batter can be prepared 24 hours ahead and refrigerated. Finished crêpes should be wrapped in foil for storage. They can be refrigerated up to 3 days, or frozen. If frozen interleave with foil, greaseproof, silicone paper or thin plastic. Reheat crêpes in foil in a 160°C/325°F/gas 3 oven for 15-20 minutes. Thaw frozen crêpes before reheating.

---

# HAM AND CHEESE CREPES

## CREPES SUISSES

Ham and cheese are two of Switzerland's finest products.

### SERVES 4 as a main course

| | |
|---|---|
| 14-16 crêpes (above) | salt and pepper |
| 1¼ pt/750 ml medium white sauce (p. 10) | ½ lb/250 g cooked ham, finely diced |
| 3 oz/75 g grated Gruyère cheese | 1 oz/25 g melted butter |
| 1 teaspoon Dijon mustard | |

Make crêpes.

Make white sauce. Take from heat and whisk in half the cheese so it melts in warm sauce. Season to taste with mustard, salt and pepper. Add half the sauce to the ham.

To finish: Fill each crêpe with a tablespoon of filling and roll like a cigar. Arrange diagonally in a shallow buttered baking dish and coat with remaining sauce. Sprinkle with melted butter and remaining grated cheese. Grill until browned and very hot. Serve in baking dish.

### GETTING AHEAD

Ham and cheese crêpes can be filled, coated with sauce and refrigerated up to 24 hours ahead, or frozen. Reheat them, uncovered, in a 160°C/325°F/gas 3 oven until very hot, 20-25 minutes. Brown them under the grill if necessary. Frozen crêpes should be thawed before reheating.

### VARIATIONS

*Broccoli Crêpes* (Crêpes aux broccolis)
Substitute ½ lb/250 g broccoli for the ham. Chop stalks coarsely and leave florets whole. Cook in boiling salted water until tender but still firm, 4-5 minutes. Drain, rinse in cold water and drain thoroughly before adding to sauce.
*Chicken Crêpes with Cheese* (Crêpes de poulet au fromage)
Substitute ½ lb/250 g cooked chicken, cut in chunks, for the ham.
*Smoked Fish Crêpes* (Crêpes au poisson fumé)
Substitute ½ lb/250 g cooked smoked fish such as haddock, mackerel or kipper for the ham.

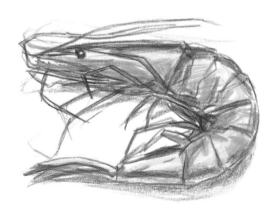

# SEAFOOD CREPES

## CREPES AUX FRUITS DE MER

Any white fish fillets can be used in this recipe, such as lemon sole, plaice, whiting or haddock.

---

### SERVES 4 as a main course

| | |
|---|---|
| *14-16 crêpes (p. 70)* | *2 oz/50 g butter* |
| *8 fl oz/250 ml white wine* | *1 oz/25 g flour* |
| *¾ pt/450 ml fish stock\** | *6 fl oz/175 ml crème* |
| *½ lb/250 g white fish fillets, cut in diagonal strips* | *fraîche\** **or** *double cream* |
| | *½ lb/250 g cooked small prawns* |
| *salt and pepper* | *juice of ½ lemon* |
| *¼ lb/125 g shelled scallops\*, quartered* | *pinch of cayenne* |

---

Make crêpes.

To cook fish: in a small saucepan boil wine until reduced by half. Add fish stock and bring to the boil. Add fish fillets, salt and pepper. Simmer until fish flakes easily with a fork, 1-2 minutes. Lift out fillets with a slotted spoon. Add scallops to liquid and simmer until just tender, about 1 minute. Lift out scallops. Strain and reserve liquid.

For sauce: in a medium saucepan, melt butter. Whisk in flour and cook until foaming, about 1 minute. Cool slightly, then whisk in reserved liquid. Bring to the boil, whisking constantly until sauce thickens. Simmer 2 minutes, add half the cream and cook 2 minutes longer.

For filling: add half the sauce to the fish fillets, scallops and prawns. Season to taste with lemon juice, salt, pepper and cayenne. Thin remaining sauce by adding remaining cream. Reheat and taste.

To finish: Fill each crêpe with a tablespoon of filling and roll like a cigar. Arrange diagonally in a shallow buttered baking dish and coat with sauce.

Grill crêpes until browned and very hot. Serve in baking dish.

### GETTING AHEAD

Seafood crêpes can be coated with sauce, then refrigerated up to 24 hours, or they can be frozen. Reheat them, uncovered, in a 160°C/325°F/gas 3 oven until very hot, 20-25 minutes. Brown them under the grill if necessary. If frozen, thaw before reheating.

### VARIATION

*Fish Crêpes* (Crêpes neptune)
Omit scallops and prawns and substitute 1 lb/500 g white fish fillets, using one or a mixture of different fish.

---

# SPINACH AND CHEESE PANNEQUETS

## PANNEQUETS AUX EPINARDS ET FROMAGE FRAIS

'Fromage frais' is best for this dish, but cottage cheese is an acceptable substitute. 'Pannequet' refers to the parcel shape in which the crêpes are folded.

---

### SERVES 4 as a main course

| | |
|---|---|
| *14-16 crêpes (p. 70)* | *grated nutmeg* |
| *1½ lb/750 g spinach* | *10 oz/300 g fromage frais* |
| *2 oz/50 g butter* | *or cottage cheese* |
| *2 spring onions or ½ large onion, chopped* | *1½ oz/40 g grated Gruyère cheese* |
| *salt and pepper* | |

---

Make crêpes.

Cook the spinach: remove stalks from fresh spinach and wash leaves thoroughly. Bring a large pan of salted water to the boil and add the spinach. When water comes back to the boil, drain the spinach and rinse it under cold water. Drain spinach thoroughly, squeezing in handfuls to extract as much water as possible. Chop spinach coarsely.

For filling: melt half the butter in a large sauté pan. Add onions and sauté until soft but not brown. Stir in spinach with salt, pepper and nutmeg. Cook, stirring, until dry, 2-3 minutes. Take from heat, stir in fromage frais or cottage cheese. Taste for seasoning.

To finish: set oven to 180°C/350°F/gas 4. Fill each crêpe with a tablespoon of the filling and fold like envelopes, turning in the ends. Arrange in a buttered baking dish. Sprinkle top with grated cheese and remaining butter, melted. Bake in oven until hot and browned, 15-20 minutes. Serve in baking dish.

### GETTING AHEAD

Crêpes can be filled and refrigerated up to 24 hours ahead, or frozen. Reheat them, uncovered, in a 160°C/325°F/gas 3 oven until very hot, 25-30 minutes. If frozen, thaw before reheating.

### VARIATION

*Onion and Cheese Pannequets* (Pannequets aux oignons et fromage)
Omit the spinach. Melt 1½ oz/40 g butter in a saucepan, add 4 large onions, thinly sliced, with salt and pepper and press a piece of foil on top. Cook, stirring occasionally, until onions are very soft but not brown, 15-20 minutes. Let cool slightly before adding cheese.

# GREEN BEAN CREPES

## CREPES DE HARICOTS VERTS

A colourful accompaniment for roast meats.

### MAKES 6-8 CREPES

| | |
|---|---|
| 2 oz/50 g green beans | salt and pepper |
| 1 oz/25 g butter | grated nutmeg |
| 1½ oz/40 g flour | pinch of cayenne |
| 1 egg | 2 tablespoons olive oil |
| 4 fl oz/125 ml milk | |

String the beans. Cook them in a large pan of boiling salted water until just tender, 5-10 minutes depending on size of beans. Drain, rinse them with cold water and drain thoroughly. Purée beans in a food processor or work through a sieve. Melt butter in a saucepan and cook purée, stirring until dry.

For the batter: sift flour into a bowl, add egg and whisk until smooth. Whisk in milk, followed by bean purée. Add salt, pepper, nutmeg and cayenne to taste.

To fry crêpes: in a crêpe pan heat a little of the oil. Add 2 tablespoons batter to the pan and fry until light brown on each side, 1-2 minutes. Do not overcook or crêpe will lose its bright green colour. Stack crêpes in a pile and keep warm in a low oven while frying remaining mixture.

### GETTING AHEAD
Batter can be prepared up to 6 hours ahead. After frying, crêpes can be kept hot in a low oven for 10-15 minutes. They can be refrigerated up to 3 days or frozen. Reheat crêpes in foil in a 160°C/325°F/gas 3 oven for 15-20 minutes. If frozen, thaw first.

### VARIATION
*Spinach Crêpes* (Crêpes aux épinards)
Substitute 2 oz/50 g spinach for green beans.

Remove stalks from fresh spinach and wash leaves thoroughly. Bring a large pan of salted water to the boil and add the spinach. When water comes back to the boil, drain the spinach and rinse under cold water. Drain spinach thoroughly, squeezing in handfuls to extract as much water as possible. Chop the spinach coarsely.

# CORN PANCAKES

## CREPES DE MAIS

A favourite accompaniment to game and pork.

### MAKES 12-15 PANCAKES

| | |
|---|---|
| 2 ears fresh sweetcorn or 7 oz/198 g can of corn niblets, drained | 2 tablespoons chopped parsley |
| 2 eggs | salt and pepper |
| 2 tablespoons flour | 2 oz/50 g butter |
| 1 teaspoon baking powder | |

Cook the ears of fresh corn in boiling water until just tender, 5-8 minutes. Drain and cut kernels from the cob with a sharp knife. Beat eggs until mixed and stir in the flour, baking powder, corn, parsley and salt and pepper to taste. Melt butter and stir in 1 tablespoon.

To fry crêpes: heat remaining butter in a large frying pan over medium heat and drop in tablespoonfuls of mixture in mounds, leaving enough space between them to turn easily. Flatten them slightly and then leave to brown first on one side and then on the other, 2-4 minutes on each side. Keep crêpes warm in a low oven while frying remaining mixture. Serve them at once.

### GETTING AHEAD
Batter can be prepared 1-2 hours ahead, but baking powder should be stirred in just before frying.

# 10
# QUICHES

When I was a child, quiche Lorraine was called bacon and egg pie and it came from my Yorkshire aunt's kitchen. Sometime in my teens it changed name and acquired status as a symbol of French cuisine. Now quiche is part of the English language. No longer restricted to bacon, quiches are flavoured with shellfish, vegetables and herbs.

Yet it is hard to improve on the classic quiche filled with a custard of whole eggs and milk. Standard proportions are 3 eggs to ¾ pt/450 ml of milk. For a richer mixture, one whole egg may be replaced by two egg yolks, and part or all of the milk by cream. As with any custard, cooking must be gentle so the eggs do not curdle; a temperature of 190°C/375°F gas 5 is ideal. Nor must the quiche be overcooked; the custard is done as soon as it is set and browned. Some cooks test by inserting a skewer to see if it comes out dry, but I simply give the quiche a little shake. It should wobble, but only slightly, like a jelly. A watery, granular custard is a sign of overcooking.

The other delicate step in cooking a quiche is to ensure that the bottom crust is crisp. Liquid custard naturally tends to make dough soggy, so the shell should be partially baked before the filling is added. A further precaution is to set the quiche tin in the oven on a baking sheet which has been preheated. Cooking gets off to a quick start and the custard has less time to soak into the pastry.

Several types of flan tins in porcelain or metal are sold specially for quiches. However pastry does not cook properly in porcelain, and with tins in one piece, the quiche cannot be lifted out easily and will tend to become soggy as it cools. Best are the French tins with a removable base which can be pushed up to free the sides.

Custard is the characteristic part of a quiche, but it acts only as the background for vigorous flavourings like ham, onion or the bacon and cheese of quiche Lorraine. Shrimps, crab, smoked fish, mushrooms cooked down to a purée, spinach – all are excellent flavourings for quiche. I like to add chopped herbs, particularly chives, as their onion taste blends well with custard. Normally flavourings are always cooked beforehand, then they are spread in the precooked pastry shell, and the custard poured on top.

That is the classic concept, but quiche is still evolving. The amount of custard may be reduced, as in quiche of Mediterranean vegetables, where courgettes or broccoli can be used in substantial quantities, thanks to their mild flavour.

When baked, it is a good idea to let a quiche stand five minutes or so before unmoulding. For maximum flavour, serve it tepid or at room temperature – avoid a scalding quiche from the oven or a chilled quiche from the refrigerator. Quiches neither freeze nor store well. Left at room temperature for a few hours, then warmed in the oven, a quiche is fine, but the refrigerator kills its subtlety. So when preparing a quiche ahead it is best to pre-bake the pastry shell and cook the flavouring separately, then assemble and bake the quiche as late as possible.

# BACON AND CHEESE QUICHE

## QUICHE LORRAINE

The classic of classics.

### SERVES 6-8

*pre-baked 10 in/25 cm pastry shell\**

| | |
|---|---|
| 4 oz/125 g bacon, diced | 3 eggs |
| 2 teaspoons oil | ¾ pt/450 ml milk |
| 1½ oz/40 g grated Gruyère cheese | salt and pepper |
| | pinch grated nutmeg |

Prepare and bake pastry shell. Heat a baking sheet in a 190°C/375°F/gas 5 oven.

Sauté bacon in oil until brown and drain on paper. Spread bacon in prepared shell with the grated cheese. Note: Both the pastry shell and bacon should be cool, otherwise they will melt the cheese.

In a bowl whisk eggs lightly and stir in milk. Add salt, pepper and nutmeg. Taste, bearing in mind the saltiness of bacon. Pour custard into shell. Bake on heated baking sheet until set and browned, 25-30 minutes. Remove quiche from oven and cool slightly before unmoulding. The filling will shrink as it cools. Serve hot or at room temperature.

### GETTING AHEAD

Pastry shell and bacon can be prepared up to 24 hours ahead. Make custard and bake quiche shortly before serving.

### VARIATION

*Onion Quiche* (Quiche aux oignons)
Substitute 1½ lb/750 g thinly sliced mild onions for bacon and cheese. In a pan melt 1 oz/25 g butter, add onions, salt and pepper. Cover tightly and cook over very low heat, stirring occasionally until they are soft and limp, but not brown, 20-25 minutes. Taste onions for seasoning, allow to cool and spread them in pre-baked pastry shell. Add custard and bake.

# INDIVIDUAL HAM QUICHES

## PETITES QUICHES AU JAMBON

This simple mixture needs the flavour of good country ham, or raw smoked ham like Italian prosciutto or Ardennes ham from Belgium.

### SERVES 6

| | |
|---|---|
| 6 pre-baked individual pastry shells\*, 4 in/10 cm in diameter | 6 fl oz/175 ml crème fraîche\* or double cream |
| 4 oz/125 g cooked country ham or raw smoked ham | 1 teaspoon Dijon mustard |
| | 1 tablespoon chopped chives (optional) |
| 2 eggs | salt (optional) and pepper |

Prepare and bake pastry shells. Heat a baking sheet in a 190°C/375°F/gas 5 oven.

Finely chop ham, discarding any fat. Spread ham in prepared shells.

For the custard: whisk eggs just until mixed. Stir in cream, mustard, chives (if using) and pepper. Taste for seasoning; salt may not be needed if ham is salty.

Set shells on heated baking sheet and pour custard into them. Cook until set and lightly browned, 15-20 minutes. Take quiches from oven and leave in tins to cool slightly before unmoulding them. Serve hot or at room temperature.

### GETTING AHEAD

Shells can be baked 1-2 days ahead. Chop the ham and mix custard just before baking the quiches.

### VARIATIONS

*Individual Anchovy Quiches* (Petites quiches aux anchois)
Omit ham and chives. Dice 2 slices bread, discarding crusts, and sauté in 1 tablespoon butter mixed with 2 tablespoons oil until golden brown, stirring constantly. Drain croûtons on absorbent paper.

Chop 8-10 anchovy fillets and spread in baked pastry shells with croûtons. Add custard and bake.

*Individual Smoked Fish Quiches* (Petites quiches au poisson fumé)

For ham, substitute the same weight of any smoked fish, such as salmon, mackerel, trout or kipper.

---

# QUICHE OF MEDITERRANEAN VEGETABLES

### QUICHE DE LEGUMES MEDITERRANEENS

Be careful not to overcook the vegetables in this quiche, so they retain their texture.

---

### SERVES 8

| | |
|---|---|
| pre-baked 10 in/25 cm pastry shell* | salt and pepper |
| 3 tablespoons olive oil | 1 small aubergine |
| 1 small onion, finely chopped | 2 medium courgettes |
| 2 cloves garlic, crushed | 1 1/2 oz/40 g grated Gruyère cheese |
| bouquet garni* | **For custard** |
| 1 1/2 lb/750 g tomatoes, peeled, seeded and chopped* | 2 eggs |
| | 4 fl oz/125 ml double cream |

---

Prepare and bake pastry shell. Heat a baking sheet in a 190°C/375°F/gas 5 oven.

In a sauté pan heat a tablespoon of the oil and sauté onion until soft but not brown, 5-7 minutes. Add garlic, bouquet garni, salt, pepper and tomatoes and simmer, stirring occasionally, until a thick purée is formed, 15-20 minutes. Taste for seasoning and leave to cool.

Meanwhile, peel aubergine and cut into thick julienne* strips. Wash courgettes and cut also into julienne strips. Heat another tablespoon of oil in a sauté pan, add aubergine, salt and pepper. Cook just until soft, 1-2 minutes. Take out and cook courgettes in remaining oil in the same way. Allow vegetables to cool.

Discard bouquet garni from the tomato purée and spread purée in prepared shell. Top with aubergines and courgettes.

For the custard: whisk eggs just until mixed and stir in cream, salt and pepper. Spoon custard over vegetables, pushing them slightly apart so custard runs through them, and sprinkle with grated cheese. Bake quiche on heated baking sheet until brown and custard is set, 15-20 minutes. Let cool slightly, and then unmould. Serve at room temperature.

### GETTING AHEAD

Pastry shell can be baked and vegetables can be cooked up to 24 hours ahead and refrigerated. Add them to shell, make custard and bake just before serving.

# 11
# HOT SAVOURY SOUFFLES

I have to confess to a partiality for soufflés. I enjoy eating them and I enjoy making them even more, for they don't take long and the return in terms of dramatic effect is high. The word means 'puffed up' and a soufflé does indeed swell up in the oven to a puffy, golden-brown castle, thanks to whipped egg whites which are combined with the basic mixture. Most popular is cheese, but savoury soufflés can also be made with puréed or flaked fish and meat or vegetables. They are usually served to open a meal or as accompaniment to the main course, though they can form a light main dish.

Whatever the mixture, it must be highly flavoured – to compensate for the neutral egg whites – and it must be cohesive, so the egg whites do not separate. Most savoury soufflés are bound with thick white sauce, or with flour, and some of the yolks from the eggs are added for richness. A few recipes omit the flour – the soufflé is more ethereal, but a good deal trickier to mix.

Strong rich flavours are important in a savoury soufflé and it is hard to beat old favourites like cheese, shellfish, mushroom and spinach. I've had soufflés based on the common onion and on such exotica as sea urchins. Mixtures like ham and broccoli can be good and you'll find that grated cheese often highlights the taste of fish or vegetables. When using vegetable purées, it is important to heat them thoroughly in butter to remove excess moisture. Meat and fish should be finely chopped or flaked so their weight cannot hold the soufflé down.

The other element in a soufflé is egg whites. When whipped, their volume should be at least double (and sometimes up to four times) that of the basic mixture. Whites for whipping should be at room temperature. They will not rise if they are contaminated with fat or water; beware of any trace of egg yolk or of moisture from a damp bowl. Metal bowls are preferable for whisking and purists insist that a copper bowl and accompanying balloon whisk are best of all. (Just before use, a copper bowl must be rubbed with a mixture of coarse salt and vinegar, then thoroughly washed and dried.) There's no doubt that copper gives plenty of volume and an excellent, close texture, yet the results of an electric mixer are quite acceptable provided it is equipped with a metal bowl and a balloon whisk.

By hand or by machine, start whisking slowly to break up the whites, then beat faster, lifting up the whisk to incorporate air. Finally whisk at full speed to tighten the egg whites into the finest possible bubbles. When ready, the whites should form flat peaks when the whisk is lifted; tall, trailing peaks mean the whites need more beating.

Once whisked, egg whites must be used at once. Add about a quarter of the egg whites to the basic mixture and stir well with a metal spoon. The mixture should be warm, just hot to the touch, so it cooks the whites slightly. This first addition of egg whites softens and lightens the basic mixture, making it easy to fold into the rest. Then tip the mixture back into the bowl of egg whites and fold the two

together as gently as possible, cutting across the middle of the mixture and scooping under and around the side with a metal spoon. Overmixing at this stage is fatal. If the egg whites start to liquify, stop folding.

The classic soufflé dish is round, with high straight sides so the mixture rises vertically as it expands. The traditional material is white glazed porcelain, fluted on the outside to resemble a pleated paper case. Alternatives are glass and earthenware and, at a pinch, any straight-sided tin or mould, such as a charlotte mould, can be used. To ensure the soufflé mixture slips up the sides without sticking, the dish must be thoroughly buttered. If the soufflé sticks, it will boil over one side and spill. (To guard against this, some cooks wrap a foil collar around the dish but I do not usually bother.) The soufflé will also spill if the dish is filled to the brim – a prudent limit is ½ in/1 cm below the rim.

Once baked, a soufflé must go at once to the table. However, there are stages during preparation when it can wait. The basic flavoured mixture can be made up to 24 hours ahead if it is tightly covered and chilled. After the egg whites have been added and the soufflé is in the mould, I've found that an hour in the refrigerator does no harm provided the mixture contains flour to bind it.

A high cooking temperature, around 200°C/400°F/gas 6 is usual for a soufflé, though in fact a mixture which is well prepared will sooner or later rise at almost any temperature. You can reckon that soufflés cooked in individual dishes will take about half as long as a large one. High heat gives a soufflé a quick boost, so the egg whites expand well before the mixture cooks and browns on the outside. The centre may be left soft, or cooked until firm, depending on individual taste. Half the charm of a cheese soufflé is the sauce formed by the soft centre, contrasting with the firm outside. Heavier mixtures of fish and vegetables should be more thoroughly cooked; to compensate for any dryness, such soufflés may be served with a sauce.

When ready, a soufflé should have increased to almost double its original volume (the heavier the mixture, the less it rises). The outside will be golden brown, with a slightly concave top. If you like a soft interior, the soufflé should wobble slightly when gently shaken. When underdone a soufflé is sloppy and will not hold up well; if overdone it is dry and tough. As a rough guide, a soufflé for four takes 15-20 minutes, and individual ones 8-12 minutes. Timing the perfect soufflé is a matter of judgement – a skill which brings an ample reward.

# CHEESE SOUFFLE

## SOUFFLE AU FROMAGE

For this cheese soufflé, any firm grating cheese such as Gruyère or Parmesan may be used. Try combining two different cheeses for a more interesting effect.

**SERVES 4 as a main dish or 6 as a first course or accompaniment to main course**

| | |
|---|---|
| 8 fl oz/250 ml thick white sauce (p. 10) | 1 teaspoon Dijon mustard |
| 4 egg yolks | salt and pepper |
| 1½ oz/40 g grated Gruyère or Parmesan cheese | 6 egg whites |
| | 1 tablespoon grated Parmesan cheese (for sprinkling) |

Make white sauce. Beat in egg yolks, one by one. Cook mixture over low heat, stirring constantly, until sauce thickens slightly, showing that egg yolks are cooked. Take from heat and stir in cheese and mustard. Reheat gently until cheese melts but do not boil or it will cook into strings. Take from heat and taste for seasoning. Note: Mixture should be highly seasoned to compensate for blandness of egg whites. Rub a piece of butter on surface of hot mixture to prevent a skin forming.

Thickly butter a 2½ pt/1.5 litre soufflé dish. Set oven to 200°C/400°F/gas 6.

Stiffly whip egg whites. Reheat cheese mixture over low heat, stirring until just hot to the touch.

Add about a quarter of egg whites to mixture and stir to combine thoroughly. Add this mixture back to remaining egg whites and fold together as lightly as possible.

Pour soufflé mixture into the prepared dish and smooth top with a metal spatula. Run your thumb around edge of mixture to make a groove which will allow the centre to rise in a high cap. Sprinkle soufflé with Parmesan and bake in oven until puffed and brown, 15-20 minutes. Serve at once.

## GETTING AHEAD

The cheese mixture can be prepared 24 hours ahead, covered tightly and refrigerated. Egg whites must be whipped and combined with hot cheese mixture not more than an hour before cooking.

## VARIATIONS

*Broccoli Soufflé (Soufflé aux broccolis)*
Reduce cheese to 1 oz/25 g. Cook 1 lb/500 g broccoli florets and stalks in boiling salted water until tender, 5-7 minutes. Drain, rinse with cold water and drain thoroughly. Purée in a food processor, or finely chop with a knife. Melt 1 oz/25 g butter in a saucepan, add broccoli and cook, stirring, until dry. Stir into thick white sauce with the cheese. Serve soufflé with fish, poultry or veal.

*Carrot Soufflé (Soufflé aux carottes)*
Reduce cheese to 1 oz/25 g. Put 1 lb/500 g sliced carrots in cold salted water and boil until very tender, 10-12 minutes. Drain and purée in a food processor or work them through a sieve. Melt 1 oz/25 g butter in a saucepan, add carrot purée and cook, stirring, until stiff enough to hold a shape. Stir into thick white sauce with the cheese. Serve soufflé with roast meats.

*Courgette Soufflé (Soufflé aux courgettes)*
Omit the cheese. Coarsely grate 1 lb/500 g courgettes, including skins. Melt 1 oz/25 g butter in a sauté pan, add 1 chopped onion and cook until soft but not browned, 5-7 minutes. Using a cloth, squeeze excess moisture from courgettes and add to the onion with 1 crushed garlic clove, salt and pepper. Cook, stirring until courgettes are tender but still firm, 1-2 minutes. Stir in 2 tablespoons chopped parsley. Add to thick white sauce instead of cheese. Serve soufflé with daube of lamb (p. 46), beef or roast chicken.

*Fish Soufflé (Soufflé de poisson)*
Omit the cheese. To thick white sauce, add ¾ lb/375 g cooked flaked fish such as salmon, cod, sea bass, whiting or smoked haddock. Beat with a wooden spatula until mixture is very smooth, 2-3 minutes. Stir in 2-3 tablespoons single cream or milk. Bake soufflé at 190°C/375°F/gas 5 until firm in the centre, 20-25 minutes. Serve with tomato velouté (p. 12), hollandaise (p. 19) or white butter sauce (p. 19).

*Shellfish Soufflé (Soufflé aux fruits de mer)*
Reduce cheese to 1 oz/25 g. To thick white sauce add ½ lb/250 g cooked flaked or chopped shellfish such as lobster, prawns or crabmeat and 2-3 tablespoons single cream or milk at the same time as the cheese. Bake soufflé at 190°C/375°F/gas 5 until firm in the centre, 20-25 minutes. Serve with hollandaise or white butter sauce (p. 19).

*Spinach Soufflé (Soufflé aux épinards)*
Reduce cheese to 1 oz/25 g. Thoroughly wash 1 lb/500 g fresh spinach, discarding stalks. Put in a large pan of boiling salted water, bring the water back to the boil and drain. Press spinach with your hands to squeeze out all water. Finely chop it and add to thick white sauce with the cheese. Season mixture with nutmeg. Serve soufflé with fish, poultry or meats.

*Turnip Soufflé (Soufflé aux navets)*
Omit cheese. Put 1 lb/500 g sliced turnips in cold salted water and boil until tender, 10-12 minutes. Drain and purée in a food processor or work them through a sieve. Melt 1 oz/25 g butter in a saucepan, add turnip purée and cook, stirring, until stiff enough to hold a shape. Stir into thick white sauce and season, adding a teaspoon of sugar if mixture tastes bitter. Serve soufflé with duck or game.

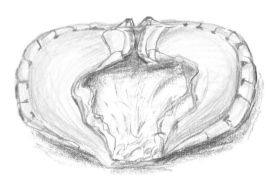

# MUSHROOM SOUFFLE

## SOUFFLE AUX CHAMPIGNONS

This recipe is based on a purée of mushrooms flavoured with shallots and parsley, known in classic French cuisine as a 'duxelles'. Serve the soufflé as a first course, or, if you like, as an accompaniment to fish, poultry or veal.

### SERVES 6

| | |
|---|---|
| *1 oz/25 g butter* | *2 tablespoons flour* |
| *1 small onion, finely chopped* | *12 fl oz/350 ml single cream* |
| *½ lb/250 g mushrooms, finely chopped* | *3 egg yolks* |
| *2 shallots, finely chopped* | *1 tablespoon chopped parsley* |
| *pinch grated nutmeg* | *6 egg whites* |
| *salt and pepper* | |

In a sauté pan melt butter and cook onion over low heat until soft but not brown, 5-7 minutes. Stir in mushrooms, shallots, nutmeg, salt and pepper and cook over medium heat until all moisture has evaporated, 4-5 minutes. Stir occasionally.

Stir in flour, add cream and bring to the boil, stirring constantly. Simmer 2 minutes. Take from heat and beat in egg yolks, one by one. Heat gently until mixture thickens slightly, showing that egg yolks are cooked. Take from heat, stir in parsley and taste. Rub surface of mixture with a lump of butter to prevent a skin forming.

Thickly butter a 2½ pt/1.5 litre soufflé dish. Set oven at 200°C/400°F/gas 6.

Stiffly whip egg whites. Reheat mushroom mixture over low heat, stirring, until just hot to the touch.

Add about a quarter of the egg whites to mixture and stir to combine. Add this mixture back to the remaining egg whites and fold together as lightly as possible.

Pour soufflé mixture into prepared soufflé dish and smooth top with a metal spatula. Run your thumb around edge to make a groove, so the centre will rise in a high cap.

Bake soufflé in oven until puffed and brown, 15-20 minutes. Serve at once.

### GETTING AHEAD

Mushroom mixture can be prepared 24 hours ahead and refrigerated. Whip egg whites and combine with hot mixture not more than an hour before baking.

### VARIATIONS

*Mushroom and Ham Soufflé (Soufflé savoyarde)*
Add ¼ lb/125 g finely chopped cooked ham or smoked ham to mushroom mixture and omit parsley. Serve as a first course.

*Mushroom Soufflé with Garlic (Soufflé aux champignons à l'ail)*
Add 1 crushed clove garlic with the shallots. Serve with steak or roast meats.

# SOUFFLE OF SCALLOPS

## SOUFFLE DE COQUILLES ST JACQUES

A food processor or blender is indispensable for this recipe. No flour is needed as the mixture is held together by a purée of raw scallops thickened with egg whites. Serve the soufflé with hollandaise or white butter sauce (p. 19) to which 2-3 teaspoons chopped chives have been added for extra flavour and colour. The delicate flavour of the scallops is well suited to this very light soufflé.

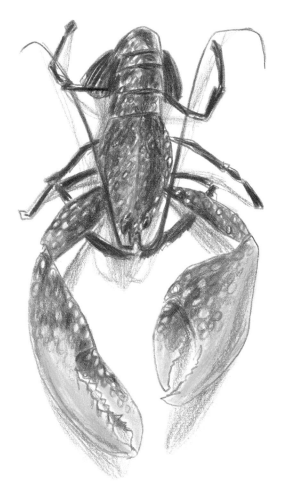

---

### SERVES 4

| | |
|---|---|
| 1½ lb/750 g shelled scallops* | 6 fl oz/175 ml crème fraîche* **or** double cream |
| 4 egg whites | salt and pepper |

---

Coarsely chop the scallops.

Whip 1½ egg whites until frothy. In a food processor or blender, purée 2-3 tablespoons scallops with 2-3 tablespoons cream and a tablespoon egg white. Turn into a bowl and repeat until all the scallops, cream and egg white are used.

Set bowl of scallop mixture over ice and beat in salt and pepper to taste. Chill thoroughly for at least 1 hour.

Thickly butter the soufflé dish and preheat oven to 180°C/350°F/gas 4.

Stiffly whip remaining egg whites. Fold a quarter into the scallop mixture. Add this mixture back to the remaining egg whites and fold together as lightly as possible. Spoon into a prepared 1¾ pt/1 litre soufflé dish and smooth top with a metal spatula.

Cook in a water bath* until brown and firm in the centre, 30-40 minutes. Serve at once, with a chive hollandaise or butter sauce.

### GETTING AHEAD

The iced scallop mixture can be kept up to 6 hours in the refrigerator. After whipped egg whites have been added, the soufflé must be baked at once.

### VARIATION

*Lobster Soufflé* (Soufflé de homard)
Substitute raw lobster meat for scallops. After puréeing lobster with cream and egg white, work it through a sieve to remove fibres. If lobster claws are available, simmer 2 claws for 8-10 minutes in salted water. Drain them, crack and extract the meat. Slice the claws in half lengthwise, and set on top of soufflé just before serving.

# —— 12 ——
# SAVOURY OMELETTES

Omelettes offer plenty of variety, from the common rolled kind, to heartier flat omelettes, laden with vegetables, bacon or sautéed croûtons and the like, and soufflé omelettes that are fluffy with whipped egg whites. When I was a student, regaling visitors on anything quick and inexpensive, omelettes were an invaluable standby. All I needed was eggs, salt, pepper and a good pan. Omelette pans can be made of aluminium, cast iron or stainless steel; and the base must be thick to distribute the heat evenly. When new, iron omelette pans should be proved*. Size of pan is important too, as the eggs for an omelette should cook quickly, but not in such a thin layer that they resemble a crêpe. A 7 in/18 cm pan is right for a 2-3 egg omelette, which will serve one person. For two, 4-5 eggs are needed with a 9 in/23 cm pan, while a big 10-11 in/ 25-28 cm pan takes 8-10 eggs for four people.

To prevent the eggs from sticking (and they stick very easily) an omelette pan should ideally be reserved for omelettes and never washed, but wiped dry while still warm with a cloth or paper towels.

There are several rules to making a successful omelette. The eggs must be fresh and they should be whisked until just mixed but not too frothy. Seasoning is added just before cooking as salt breaks down egg white, making the omelette tough. All omelettes should be cooked over brisk heat but not so fierce that the eggs scorch. An omelette that is cooked too fast is both tough and charred; cooked too slowly, however, it will be flat and pale. Ten eggs are

a maximum to cook in a single omelette.

A hot omelette should, of course, be eaten at once, but most omelettes are also good eaten cold, sliced in wedges or sandwiched in French bread. Cold omelettes can also be layered in a buttered gratin dish with a tomato sauce, sprinkled with grated cheese and baked in the oven until heated through.

## FLAT OMELETTES

Flat omelettes tend to have a lower proportion of eggs to other ingredients – the eggs act simply as a binding agent. The method of cooking a flat omelette depends on its thickness. If thin, cook the bottom over a brisk heat, then flip with a spatula and brown the other side. For thicker flat omelettes, cook one side, slide the omelette onto a plate and flip it back into the pan. Alternatively the top can be grilled until brown.

## ROLLED OMELETTES

A rolled omelette requires only eggs, butter, salt and pepper, though a few finely chopped herbs or a sprinkling of grated cheese is a welcome addition. The outside of the perfect omelette is golden brown and the inside is runny, never firm. Depending on the number of eggs, cooking should take only ½ to 1 minute. Rolled omelettes tend to be lighter than flat omelettes, and should have more delicate flavourings. One advantage of their shape is that they can be stuffed after the eggs are set – a good way of using leftover cooked vegetables. Fish in a sauce or beef bourguignon can be excellent in a rolled omelette.

# FLAT OMELETTE WITH CHEESE

## OMELETTE COMTOISE

Instead of being cooked entirely over a flame, this flat omelette is fried on one side, then browned under the grill. It is a delicious and quite substantial omelette with an attractive golden top. Serve with a salad for lunch or supper.

### SERVES 2

| | |
|---|---|
| 4-5 eggs | 3 tablespoons double |
| salt and pepper | cream |
| 1 tablespoon butter | 2 oz/50 g grated Gruyère cheese |

Light grill. In a medium bowl, whisk eggs with pepper and a little salt just until thoroughly mixed.

Heat butter in a 9 in/23 cm omelette pan over a high heat until it stops foaming and begins to brown; add eggs immediately.

Stir briskly with flat of a fork for 8-10 seconds until eggs start to thicken and then quickly pull egg that sets at sides of pan to the centre, tipping pan to pour uncooked egg to the sides. Continue until about half of egg is set.

Take from heat and spoon cream over eggs. Sprinkle with grated cheese and grill until golden.

Cut omelette in half, slide onto two plates and serve at once.

### VARIATION

*Flat Omelette with Smoked Haddock* (Omelette Arnold Bennett)

Put ¾ lb/375 g smoked haddock fillet in a saucepan and pour over 8 fl oz/250 ml milk. Cover and simmer 8-10 minutes until fish flakes easily. Let cool and drain. Flake the haddock and discard skin and bones. Put fish in a small saucepan with the cream and heat gently. Make omelettes as above, adding fish/cream mixture and cheese.

# FLAT OMELETTE WITH MUSHROOMS

## OMELETTE AUX CHAMPIGNONS

Flat omelettes always contain substantial amounts of vegetables, with just enough eggs to bind them.

### SERVES 2

| | |
|---|---|
| ¼ lb/125 g mushrooms, thinly sliced | salt and pepper |
| 1 oz/25 g butter | 1 tablespoon chopped parsley |
| ½ clove crushed garlic (optional) | 4-5 eggs |

Sauté mushrooms in half the butter with garlic until tender, 5-7 minutes. Add salt, pepper and parsley.

In a medium bowl, whisk eggs with salt and pepper just until thoroughly mixed. Stir in mushrooms.

Heat remaining butter in a 9 in/23 cm omelette pan over medium heat until it stops spluttering and begins to brown. At once add egg mixture.

Stir eggs briskly with flat of a fork and when they start to thicken continue stirring until mixture is as thick as scrambled eggs.

Let omelette cook 20-25 seconds or until well browned on the bottom and almost firm on top.

Either flip the omelette with a spatula or take the pan from the heat, set a heatproof plate on top and turn omelette onto it. Slide omelette back into the pan and brown other side.

Serve hot or cold, cut in half or in wedges.

### GETTING AHEAD

A flat omelette must be made at the last minute if it is to be eaten hot. It can be made 6-8 hours ahead to serve at room temperature.

### VARIATIONS

*Peasant Omelette* (Omelette paysanne)

Omit mushrooms. Dice ¼ lb/125 g bacon and sauté until brown. Add 2 medium potatoes, cut in dice, and continue cooking until potatoes are brown and crisp, stirring occasionally. Add pepper and 2 tablespoons chopped parsley. The bacon will provide enough salt. Stir into eggs.

*Potato Omelette* (Omelette parmentier)
Omit mushrooms. Dice 3 medium potatoes and sauté in 1½ oz/40 g butter until brown and crisp, stirring occasionally. Sprinkle with salt, pepper and 2 tablespoons chopped parsley. Stir into eggs just before cooking omelette.

*Spanish Omelette* (Omelette à l'espagnole)
Omit mushrooms. Sauté 1 thinly sliced onion in 2 tablespoons oil until soft. Add 1 red pepper and 1 green pepper (or 2 green ones), cut in thin strips, with salt, pepper and a crushed clove of garlic. Continue cooking and stirring, until peppers are soft. Taste and stir into eggs.

---

# ROLLED OMELETTE WITH HERBS

## OMELETTE AUX FINES HERBES

The classic 'fines herbes' mixture is made from equal quantities of chervil, tarragon and chives. Basil, marjoram and oregano are good too and plain parsley will do at a pinch.

---

### SERVES 2

| | |
|---|---|
| 4-5 eggs | salt and pepper |
| 2 tablespoons finely chopped fresh herbs | 1 tablespoon butter |

---

In a medium bowl, whisk eggs with salt and pepper just until thoroughly mixed. Add herbs.

Heat butter in a 9 in/23 cm omelette pan over high heat until it stops foaming and begins to brown. Add eggs immediately.

Stir briskly with flat of a fork for 8-10 seconds until eggs start to thicken, then quickly pull egg that sets at sides of pan to the centre, tipping pan to pour uncooked egg to the sides. Continue until most of egg is set, or some is still runny, according to your taste.

Leave omelette to brown without stirring for 10-15 seconds. Have a warm plate ready.

To roll omelette, hold pan handle in your left hand and tip pan away from you. Either give handle a sharp tap with your right hand so further edge of omelette flips over or fold the edge with the help of a fork. Half roll, half slide omelette onto a plate so it lands folded in three.

Pull in side of omelette with a fork to neaten it and, if you like, brush top with melted butter to give an attractive shine.

### GETTING AHEAD
Omelettes must be made at the last minute if they are to be eaten hot. Any leftovers can be stuffed into French bread to make an excellent sandwich.

### VARIATIONS
*Bacon Omelette* (Omelette au lard)
Substitute ¼ lb/125 g bacon for the herbs. Dice bacon and fry until brown, drain and add to eggs. If you like, fry the omelette in bacon fat instead of butter.

*Croûton Omelette* (Omelette aux croûtons)
Substitute 3 slices white bread for the herbs. Discard crusts and dice. Sauté in about 2 tablespoons butter, stirring constantly so the croûtons brown evenly. Drain them on paper towels and add to eggs just before cooking.

*Onion Omelette* (Omelette lyonnaise)
Use parsley instead of mixed herbs. In 1 oz/25 g butter sauté 3 very thinly sliced onions until brown. Flavour with 2 teaspoons wine vinegar, salt and pepper and stir in parsley. Fill omelette with mixture before folding.

*Vegetable Omelette* (Omelette à la jardinière)
Use parsley instead of mixed herbs. Finely dice 1 medium potato, 1 carrot and 1 stalk celery. Sauté the vegetables in 1 oz/25 g butter until soft and lightly browned. Add parsley, salt and pepper to taste. Fill omelette with vegetables before folding.

# GLOSSARY

### Arrowroot
Used to thicken sauces at the end of cooking. Arrowroot gives a lighter result than flour and the sauce is clear and glossy. Potato starch can be substituted. Cornflour gives a similar effect, but less is needed and the sauce will not be clear.

To use arrowroot: mix it in a cup or small bowl with three times its volume of cold water (or liquid such as Madeira). Stir to a soft paste. Bring liquid to the boil and whisk in arrowroot paste; the sauce will thicken at once. Add only enough paste to thicken sauce to consistency you want. Do not continue boiling, as after 5 or 10 minutes, arrowroot loses its thickness.

### Blanching
Blanching is a preliminary to cooking. Ingredients like chicken and sweetbreads are blanched (literally, whitened) but this is a narrow use of the term. Green vegetables are blanched to set their colour. Strong flavours (onion and garlic) and salt (as in bacon) are reduced by blanching. Bones for stock, are cleaned by blanching. Blanching also changes the texture of ingredients by softening or stiffening them.

### Bouquet garni
A bundle of aromatic herbs, sometimes including vegetables, used for flavouring braises, ragoûts and sauces. A bouquet garni always includes a bay leaf, a sprig of thyme (or a large pinch of dried thyme) and parsley stalks (leaves are kept for decoration). Optional additions are celery tops, a piece of leek, and herbs such as rosemary and oregano. Tie ingredients together with string so they are easy to remove.

### Carving a bird
Cut between leg and body, following outline of thigh, until leg joint is visible. With a two-pronged fork, twist leg sharply outwards to break thigh joint and pull leg forwards from body so all meat comes with it. Repeat with other leg. Cut legs in half through joint, using line of fat on underside as a guide.

To carve breast, cut horizontally through breast meat just above wing bone, through to ribs. Angling the knife, carve breast meat in diagonal slices from the bone until top of breastbone is reached and all meat is removed. Repeat on other side. Cut out 'oyster' meat from under backbone. Serve each person with a piece of leg and some slices of breast.

### Chestnuts, peeling
With a small knife make a slit at the end of each nut. Put them in a pan of cold water and bring just to the boil. Peel with a knife while still hot, lifting out a few nuts at a time. If they cool, reheat them. Remove both outer and inner skin.

### Clarified butter
Butter from which impurities, in the form of milk solids, have been removed. Clarified butter can be heated to a high temperature without burning. To clarify butter, gently heat it and cook until it splutters. Take from heat and skim foam from surface. Pour clear yellow butter into a bowl, leaving milky residue at bottom of pan. Alternatively, chill butter until set and discard residue.

### Crème fraîche
Thick, sharp-tasting cream with a high butterfat content. Crème fraîche adds piquant flavour, particularly to soups and sauces, but double cream can be used instead.

To make crème fraîche: stir together in a saucepan ¾ pt/450 ml double cream and 8 fl oz/250 ml buttermilk, sour cream or yogurt. Heat gently until almost warm to the touch, 25°C/75°F. Pour into a container and partly cover. Keep at this temperature 6-8 hours or until cream has thickened and tastes slightly acid. On a cold day it may take longer to thicken. Stir cream, cover and refrigerate. Crème fraîche will keep up to 2 weeks.

### Croûtes
Slices of bread, cut in squares, triangles, rounds or hearts and toasted or fried in butter.

For toasted croûtes: cut bread in ½ in/1 cm slices, toast, then trim in shape you want. To accompany pot-au-feu and some soups, bread is cut in rough cubes or slices, then baked in a 175°C/350°F/gas 4 oven until crisp and brown, 10-15 minutes.

For fried croûtes: slice bread and trim. In a frying pan heat enough oil to generously cover the base. Add a layer of croûtes, brown them on both sides over medium heat and drain on paper towels.

### Cutting up a raw bird
With a sharp knife, cut between leg and body, following outline of thigh until leg joint is visible. Locate 'oyster' piece of meat lying against backbone, and cut around it so it remains attached to thigh. Twist leg sharply outwards to break thigh joint. Cut forwards to detach each leg from body, including oyster meat. With a knife or poultry shears, cut away

and remove backbone. Cut along breastbone to halve the carcass. Cut off wingtips. The bird is now in 4 pieces.

To cut into 6 pieces, divide each breast in half, cutting diagonally through meat, then through breast and rib bones so a portion of breast meat is cut off with wing. Trim rib bones.

To cut into 8 pieces, cut legs in half through joint, using white line of fat on underside as guide. Trim drumsticks and any protruding bones with poultry shears.

### Fish stock

Thoroughly wash 1½ lb/750 g fish bones including heads. Drain and chop in large pieces, discarding any skin. In a large saucepan sauté 1 medium onion, sliced, in 1 tablespoon butter until soft but not brown. Add fish bones and cook until white, 1-2 minutes. Add 2 pts/1.25 litres water, 1 teaspoon peppercorns, a bouquet garni and 4 fl oz/125 ml dry white wine *or* 2 tablespoons white wine vinegar. Bring slowly to the boil, skimming often. Simmer 20 minutes. Strain stock through a fine sieve. Use at once, or let cool to room temperature before refrigerating. Makes about 1¾ pt/1 litre stock.

*Fish glaze:* for about 2 fl oz/60 ml glaze, boil 1¾ pt/1 litre fish stock until very reduced and syrupy in consistency.

### Flaming

Food is flamed in spirit or in fortified wine with a high alcohol content. After flaming, only the essence remains and food is slightly toasted. To flame: heat alcohol in a small pan, light it and pour over the hot food. Continue basting with liquid until the flame dies. If the dish contains sugar, cooking should be continued until the sugar caramelizes.

### Julienne strips, cutting

Julienne strips are matchstick length but more finely cut. For root vegetables, trim sides of vegetable to a square, then slice into 2 in/5 cm lengths. Cut lengths in thin vertical slices. Stack slices and cut in thin strips. For celery and green pepper, cut vegetable lengthwise in thin 2 in/5 cm strips.

### Larding

To thread strips of pork fat into lean cuts of meat. The fat partially dissolves by the end of cooking, helping to make meat moist and tender. To lard, cut a piece of pork fat into strips thin enough to insert in a larding needle. Sew strips into meat at regular intervals. If you have no needle, pierce meat with point of a knife and insert the strips of fat.

### Marinating

To soak food in liquid and seasonings so as to tenderize it and add flavour. A marinade contains wine, vinegar or lemon juice, so it is acid enough to break down tissues; seasonings include vegetables, herbs and spices.

The ingredients for a marinade may be stirred together to use as they are, or they may be boiled for 5 minutes and cooled before pouring over the food. A cooked marinade acts more quickly than an uncooked one. Depending on the strength of flavour wanted, marinating time can range from an hour or two for thin slices of fish to two or three days for large pieces of meat. Marinating is normally done in the refrigerator; if left at room temperature, halve the estimated time.

Never marinate in an aluminium or tinned copper pan as the marinade will acquire a metallic taste. Choose a deep container so the food is completely immersed and keep it covered, stirring or turning from time to time. After marinating, food to be browned in fat must be thoroughly dried so it sears well. The marinade liquid itself is almost always used in the recipe to make a sauce, sometimes together with the vegetables and seasonings.

### Mussels

To clean, cook and shell mussels, wash under running water, removing any weed. Discard broken shells and any mussels that do not close when tapped. Put mussels in a large pan, cover and cook over high heat, tossing occasionally, until mussels open (5-7 minutes). Reject any that remain closed. Remove mussels from shells and discard 'beard' (rubbery ring surrounding mussel).

### Plain pastry

Sift 7 oz/200 g flour onto a board or table top. With a sweep of your hand, make a large well in the centre. With your fist, pound 3½ oz/100 g cold butter until pliable. Put it in the well with 1 egg yolk, ½ teaspoon salt and 3 tablespoons cold water. Have ready more cold water and a pastry scraper or metal spatula. With your fingertips, work the butter, pinching it until mixed with egg and water. Gradually work in flour with one hand, using pastry scraper or spatula in other hand as a scoop. The mixture will form coarse crumbs. If these seem dry, add more water and continue working until dough forms a ball. Lightly flour board and blend dough for 1-2 minutes, pushing it away with the heel of your hand and gathering it up with the scraper. Dough should be pliable and peel easily from the board. Shape it into a ball, wrap and chill it at least 30 minutes before rolling. This recipe makes enough dough for a 10 in/25 cm shell or about six 3½ in/10 cm individual shells.

**Pastry shells, individual, lining and pre-baking**

*Note:* Double the number of tins are needed as one tin is used for moulding and another for lining each shell. Lightly butter half the tins. Roll dough to about ¼ in/4 mm thickness. Stamp out rounds about ½ in/1 cm larger than the tins, using a plain or fluted pastry cutter or sharp-edged tumbler. Line buttered tins with a round of pastry, pressing it well into the base and against the sides with your finger and thumb. Dough should extend above the edge of the tin to give a deep shell. Prick base of shells all over and chill until firm, 10-15 minutes. Preheat oven to 200°C/400°F/gas 6. Gently press another tin into the dough shell, so dough is held in place. The tin may be same size or slightly smaller than the shell. Set tins on a baking sheet. Bake shells in oven until edges start to brown and dough is set, 8-10 minutes. Remove upper tins and continue baking until base is dry and lightly browned, 5-7 minutes. Let cool in the tins.

**Pastry shells, large, lining and pre-baking**

Lightly butter a quiche tin. Flour a board or table top and roll dough to a circle about 2 in/5 cm larger than the tin. Dough should be about ¼ in/5 mm thick. Roll dough loosely around rolling pin, lift and unroll it over the tin. Lift edges of dough with one hand and, using a small ball of dough dipped in flour, press it well into bottom corners of tin with other hand. *Note:* do not stretch dough across base of tin or it will shrink during baking. Overlap edges of dough inside the tin. Roll rolling pin across top of tin to cut off dough. Push up dough with finger and thumb so it extends above the edge of tin, giving a deep pastry shell. Neaten edge of dough and, if you like, flute it with pastry tongs. Prick base of shell all over with a fork and chill until firm, 15-20 minutes. Preheat oven to 190°C/375°F/gas 5. Before baking shell, it must be lined with paper and weighted with beans to keep its shape. Cut a circle of greaseproof/wax paper about 3 in/7.5 cm larger than the quiche tin and crumple it. Line the shell, pressing paper well into corners and sides so dough cannot shrink. Fill paper with dried beans or rice so air bubbles cannot form underneath dough. (Beans can be stored and used again for the same purpose.) Bake shell in oven until edges start to brown and dough is set, about 15 minutes. Lift out paper and beans and continue baking until dough is dry and base is lightly browned, 6-8 minutes. Let cool in the tin.

**Proving pans**

All new iron and cast iron pans should be proved so that they do not rust or stick; it is also advisable to prove omelette and crêpe pans which have been washed.

To prove a pan: cover base with ½ in/1 cm oil and a generous handful of coarse salt. Leave overnight, then heat pan gently on top of stove or in oven until oil is very hot and almost smoking. Leave until tepid, then discard oil and salt and wipe pan dry.

**Scallops**

To prepare scallops, wash and dry them and discard crescent-shaped muscle at side of white meat.

**Skewer**

Used to test cooking of roast meat, terrines and other bulky foods. Insert a skewer in centre of the food and leave 30 seconds. Withdraw skewer and at once test temperature against your lips or back of your hand. A very hot skewer indicates heat has reached centre of food and it is well done (right for pork, ham, fish and vegetable terrines). When skewer is medium hot, the food is just cooked (right for poultry, veal and meat terrines). For rare lamb and beef the skewer should be warm. When the skewer is cold, food is not ready.

**Stock, veal brown**

Preheat oven to 230°C/450°F/gas 8. Put 4 lb/2 kg veal bones, (shin and knuckles, cracked in pieces) in a roasting pan and roast in oven until browned, stirring occasionally, 30-40 minutes. Add 2 onions, stuck with 2 cloves, 2 stalks celery and 2 carrots and continue roasting until browned, 20-30 minutes. Transfer bones and vegetables to stockpot, discarding fat. Add a bouquet garni, 1 tablespoon peppercorns and 8 pt/5 litres water (or to cover). Simmer stock uncovered 5-6 hours, skimming occasionally; it should reduce very slowly by about one third. For a well-coloured stock, add 1 tablespoon tomato purée towards end of cooking. Strain stock though a fine sieve. If flavour is not concentrated, boil it until reduced. Allow to cool to room temperature, then refrigerate. When well chilled, skim off solidified fat. Makes about 4 pt/2.5 litres stock.

*Brown beef stock:* use half beef and half veal bones.
*White veal stock:* instead of browning bones, blanch

them by putting in a large pan of cold water, bringing just to the boil and simmering 5 minutes, skimming off froth as it rises to the surface. Drain, rinse and then proceed with recipe.

*Chicken stock:* in recipe for white veal stock substitute 3 lb/1.5 kg raw chicken backs and necks for veal bones and reduce water by one third. Simmer stock 3-4 hours.

*Meat glaze:* to make about 4 fl oz/125 ml glaze, boil 4 pt/2.5 litres any of the above stocks to reduce until dark and syrupy.

## Tomatoes, peeling, seeding and chopping

With a small knife remove core from stem end of tomato and cut a small cross in the top, piercing the skin only. Lower tomatoes into boiling water 5-10 seconds (depending on ripeness), drain and peel. Cut tomatoes crosswise to expose seeds, then squeeze each half gently in palm of your hand, shaking to dislodge the seeds. Coarsely chop tomatoes with a large knife and, if you like, sieve seeds to extract juice.

## Trussing a bird

Trussing encloses any stuffing and keeps a bird in shape so it cooks evenly. Remove wishbone to make carving easier: lift neck skin and, with a small sharp knife, outline wishbone and cut it free from breastbone.

Set bird on its back on a board. Insert trussing needle through leg at joint, then through other leg, pulling string to far side of bird. Turn bird on its breast and tuck wing tip bones under bird to hold neck skin. Insert needle into wing bone on same side of bird. Stretch neck skin along backbone and catch it down with the needle. Pierce other wing with needle, pull through string and cut to free the needle. Tie ends of string tightly together at the side. Wind a second string around tail of bird and drumsticks and tie tightly.

## Water bath

Used both for cooking and keeping food warm. Water diffuses direct heat and ensures food keeps moist and does not get too hot.

To cook in a water bath, bring a deep roasting pan of water to the boil and set mould or pan of food in it; the water should come at least half way up sides of mould. Bring water back to the boil and transfer to oven at 190°C/375°F/gas 5 or continue cooking on top of stove, according to recipe. Count cooking time from moment water comes back to the boil.

To keep foods hot in a water bath: set mould or pan in a roasting pan of hot but not boiling water and leave over very low heat. The water should not boil.

# INDEX